THE KANDA ODYSSEY

In search of self

A Memoir

TIMOTHY KANDASHU MAJERO

To my mother, Agnes, and to Mother Africa. From the one womb I come and to the other, the original, I return for good. And to my wife, Rose, a great source of succor in between, and without whose insistent nagging that I had something to share, my story would have remained untold.

The difficulty is to know which self to make the permanent one and which we should leave ephemeral. You set one of the passing selves above your permanent self: that's doing violence to yourself. Things will go wrong then, and you will never know why as long as you remain in the same situation and don't move out of it.

—Ayi Kwei Armah (*The Healers*)

PROLOGUE

It is the way of nature that there is always a moment of brightness before darkness sets in. The brighter the moment, the darker the gloom that follows. It is often that we are not fully aware of the brightness itself, only to perceive it in retrospect, magnified by the contrast of the darkness. Thus, it never occurred to me that I was in paradise, and I had been, until I came face to face with living hell on earth, in the land of my birth. Darkness and horror pervade the land, and the inhabitants scramble across the shores of the nation in search of refuge. A people's savior turned monster, devouring its own subjects. And here I am, this twenty-seventh day of April 2003, agonizing over a decision I could never have ever imagined making. I love my family, and the core of my being is rooted in the land of my fathers. Yet here I am, fleeing to join the exodus, turning my back to all the things that give meaning to my life, and not knowing if and when to return or whether there would be anything left to return to. In times like these, the human instinct for survival focuses on flee-ing from harm, making the destination inconsequential. But there is some irony here, for I am headed for England! Yes, to the home of the same British who colonized my country; the same British we vilified as enemies of my people, and the same we had a long and bitter fight over our own freedom. Our 1980 African nationhood and political independence! And so here I am, giving my back to my beloved Zimbabwe, an escape from my erstwhile savior into the arms of my erstwhile enemy. Seeking refuge in the bowls of the tiger!

And so after a long interval of time, one becomes curious and wants to know; where are you at now, Kanda? Yes, indeed. Where, what, who art thou now, Kanda?

WELCOME TO THE WORLD

Born in the presence of the gods.

Kanda had a humble entry into this world. He was born in a pole and mud hut, attended to by the elderly village midwives. However, it was not his humble birth that the villagers would remember the most about Kanda's coming into the world. His two sisters before him had been born under the same conditions. It was the norm of the time. Times would change though, and his two sisters and three brothers after him would be hospital babies, tended to by doctors and nurses, all in white attire, under spotless and sterile conditions. All this was way ahead of Kanda's time, and there are no regrets. For what is regarded primitive is only so in retrospect viewed against what now is. Every moment in a people's life has its own high points, and as in this case, the elderly village midwives who helped bring Kanda into this world were the best of the times. They cut Kanda's umbilical cord and buried it into the ground behind the hut, and Kanda lived. There is a unique and profound thing about being born at the village. You get to know where your umbilical cord is buried. It gives you a sense of being truly bound to the land of your birth.

Kanda's father, Mhishi, was a staunch Christian man while most of the village continued to follow their traditional way of praying to their Mwari through their ancestors. The white missionaries who came with the colonial settlers regarded ancestral worship a heathen practice, a worship of the dead. It has never been clear whether this was some genuine misunderstanding or a deliberate intent to denigrate the African religious practice. For ancestral worship is not a worship of the dead but a prayer and devotion to the Creator through the ancestors, just as Christians and followers of other religions pray to the same Creator through human beings that once lived but are now dead. Ancestral worship is the indigenous people's prayer to God through their ancestors in the same way Christians pray to God through Christ or the Muslims through Muhammad. Instead of trying to find common ground between Christianity and the local people's religion, the white missionaries simply and contemptuously dismissed the latter as primitive and heathen, asserting that theirs was the superior and only true religion. They never sought to understand, partner, or incorporate the religious practices of the people of the land. Their notion of saving the black souls was to defile and destroy their centuries-old link with their Mwari, the universal God. And Christianity made it very clear that you were either on its side or with the devil, no double identity. It was thus that Kanda was born in the midst of two competing religions in the village.

It was in the wee hours of Wednesday, October 4, 1944, that Kanda's shrill birth cry was heard from his mother's hut. The cry, which was accompanied by excited ululation from the women, was carried by the wind into the night, much of it swallowed by the sound of the drum nearby. It was the drama of his birth amid the commotion of fervent Christian prayer as well as festive ancestral worship that the villagers would remember the most about Kanda's birth. His father had been praying most of the night from a nearby hut. His prayer had been loud and impassioned, prompting some of the women to snicker, joking that when a man prays that much, he must be asking for a son. Kanda's birth cry was heard at almost the same time that there was a burst of loud cheers accompanied by the drumbeat, clapping, and ululating a few huts up the village, where some of the villagers were conducting a *bira*, an all-night ancestral ceremony. The excitement coming from the *bira* was an indication that the ancestors had arrived. While the *bira* was an all-night worship through singing and dancing, the ancestors were only expected to appear and announce themselves through the spirit mediums at dawn. It was the timing of Kanda's birth amid the Christian prayer on the one hand and the presence of the ancestral spirits on the other that prompted the villagers to whisper among themselves, "This child is born in the presence of the gods." And some added that it was a double blessing from their Mwari and the white man's God. Kanda would, however, wonder as he grew up whether this was indeed a blessing or a curse, something that follows you everywhere like your shadow, always mocking and nagging you about your true identity.

KANDA'S BIRTHPLACE

With or without the milk and the honey, this is my own Canaan.

Kanda spent his early years at the village, a collection of home-steads of pole and mud huts nestled under the shadow of a towering Chitenga mountain to the southwest. Chitenga was home to hordes of baboons and monkeys and abundant wild fruit. Down a wooded slope to the north, the village was bounded by the Nhora River, a serene meander good for fishing and children's swimming during the dry season but a gushing and roaring torrent during the heavy summer rains. The village stretched east-west for about a kilometer, arranged in a straight fashion as ordered by the colonial rulers. The reason given for this arrangement was that it would facilitate future community development. The colonial government promised to bring roads, electricity, and running water. As everybody else knew though, there were other reasons for this arrangement of the villages. It would make it easier for the authorities to control and enforce order among the natives than if they were allowed to live as they chose, scattered all over the bush.

The village faced north, with the back reserved for crop fields, which stretched south to the edge of Mutatu farm, one of thousands of large-scale commercial farming enterprises owned by white settlers. As everywhere else, you could tell where the village lands ended and the farmland began. Much of the land in Zimbabwe, then known by its colonial name Rhodesia, was divided into large commercial farms owned exclusively by whites on the one hand and, on the other, communal living areas referred to as Native Reserves. About six thousand white settlers owned almost half of the land, with the remainder comprised of state land and the Native Reserves. The farms were characterized by the best soils in areas of good rains or other sources of water, while the Native Reserves were located in arid, sandy soils. Mutatu farm was such a neighbor to the south.

On the other side, between the homesteads and the river, were the cattle pens. While herding cattle and goats during the day was communal and done in turns, each family had its own pen and was responsible for the safety of its animals at night. A passing stranger would be able to tell the status of the different families by the size of their herd. Less well-to-do families would only have a few goats to their name or nothing at all.

Across the Nhora River was a wide patch of grazing land, running parallel to the river, merging to the north into a vast forest extending far north to Chemhofu Mountain, notorious for its bogeyman who preyed on stray children. There were dotted patches of grazing land within the vast bushy area.

To the west of the village was an adjoining smaller village, Ndoro, and a short distance from there, the nearest school, Gorwa, a Salvation Army school, a kilometer away from Kanda's village. To get to the other villages on the east, one had to cross the Nhora River, now running southeast toward the larger Mubvinzi River. Just across the river was a wooded area that opened up to a grassy plain before reaching the first two villages, Sika and Mavunga, leading up to the other local school, Chindotwe, a Methodist Church school five kilometers away.

For most of Kanda's early life, these surroundings were his habitat, his world. Even in later years, it is a place that has remained the center of his universe, a Mecca that he, from time to time, returns to, both spiritually and physically, to recharge and reorient. A place he calls his Canaan, with or without the milk and the honey.

Kanda's village is situated in Msana Communal Land, then known as Msana Native Reserve. Msana is a mountainous country, its name an apt depiction of this feature. In Kanda's native language, *msana* means the back, as in the rear part of a human body or the back of a horse. As a little child, Kanda used to think of his part of the country as the back of the world, rising above all else, way up like the hump of the camel, with the rest of the world sloping down toward the horizon. In his little mind, he was proud to be on top of the world. And it is here, on this tiny spot in the universe, the raised hump of his little world, that Kanda views the rest of the larger world in his endeavor to define and find his place in it.

VILLAGE CHILDHOOD

Love, innocence, and nature.

Some of Kanda's memories of his early life are faint and blurred, coming back slowly like the vision of the sun gradually breaking through the early spring morning mist before reaching full view, bright and warm. While not fully defined, these memories are, however, wrapped in feelings of warmth and happiness, suggesting that the sun must have been bright and warm even behind the mist, beyond the reach of Kanda's recall. An early childhood vaguely remembered, but one of happiness.

Kanda's family was considered well-to-do by local community standards. They were what would perhaps now be regarded as middle class, with people such as the chief, the police, the teachers, and the businessmen regarded as the elite. They had a sizable herd of cattle, a plough, and the only ox-drawn cart and bicycle in the village. Both his parents had several years of primary education and were able to read and write. Both were prominent and respected members of their local Methodist Church, and his father was a lay preacher and a well-known political activist. The whole family went to church on Sundays. Kanda's father was a licensed heavy vehicle driver, but his employment in the city was on and off due to a chronic leg problem. When he was at the village, he raised money from his large garden, where he grew a variety of crops and vegetables for sale in the city. He also ordered and sold other produce from the surrounding commercial farms. The family was well provided for with adequate food and clothing, and when the children were of age, they went to school. Kanda's father took care of the elderly, the widowed, and the disabled of the village.

Kanda's mother was a hardworking woman and was very particular about hygiene and cleanliness. She was the best cook Kanda has ever known. Kanda will never forget the story of one of his cousins who, after sharing a meal with him, declared to Kanda's mother that, "*Ndiro sadza randinodaka iri, haikona rinobikwa na amai vangu!*" meaning, "This is the *sadza* I like, not the kind cooked by my mother!" *Sadza* is the local staple food made of maize meal and is eaten with a relish such as meat, vegetables, fish. Kanda and his siblings were close-knit and well-behaved.

Childhood in the village developed in stages. The early stages are spent with mother and siblings, followed by tentative ventures outside the home with neighboring children. At about age three, a child starts to tag along behind older siblings to other parts of the village, to the fields, or to the river. With time, the child becomes part of the larger village. Initially all the children play together before they slowly separate into distinct age groups whose activities are determined by whether one was a boy or a girl. Much of this time is a period of innocence, surrounded by family and loved ones and shielded from the demands of growing up yet to come.

People that loom large in Kanda's childhood memories, aside from his immediate family, are Tobias, his cousin and best childhood friend; Auntie D, his mother's younger sister; and *Mbuyanhini*, his grandfather's youngest wife. Tobias's parents were divorced, and he and his two younger brothers and a sister lived with their mother (who was Kanda's father's half-sister) at the village. He and Kanda were inseparable. It was with Tobias that Kanda first learned to swim, to fish, to shoot birds, and to make traps to catch mice, birds, fish, and rabbits. They had much fun, alone together most of the time. Both were well-behaved and did not get into much trouble, except for the occasional time Grandpa caught them helping themselves to some mangoes in his orchard.

Kanda and Tobias also participated in many other activities with the other village children. They went to different schools and would link up in the evenings and on weekends after work in the fields and other home chores. These were happy times, until one day, when Tobias was about twelve years old. His father came from neighboring Chikwaka Reserve to claim his custody. There had been failed attempts before, but this time, his father was determined to take his son to the home of his fathers. His father came very early in the morning and found Tobias at home inside the house. Tobias was caught by surprise, and there was nowhere to run as he had before. After trying everything he could think of to resist with no success, he removed all his clothes, believing that his father would not take him out of the house naked. Grabbing Tobias in one hand and carrying the small bundle of his clothes in the other, the father dragged him out naked, down along the length of the village, with Tobias screaming, kicking, and scratching. Kanda and the other children came out of their houses to watch sadly, until both disappeared from view. The two friends would not see each other again for many years. They met briefly as grown-ups before Tobias passed away from injuries sustained at the hands of the Rhodesian security forces during the war of liberation for Zimbabwe.

For Kanda and the other kids, Christmas was special, the best time of the year. Not so much for its religious significance but for the goodies that came with it. Everybody was happy and in a generous mood. Only the best food was laid out for the day. Kanda's father would come from the city with fresh bread, condensed milk, butter, and sugar for breakfast. The specialty for lunch and dinner was always rice and chicken. Organic wholesome rice or the rich brown rice, plain or laced with peanut butter. And the chicken was always the real deal, a road runner fattened for the occasion. Kanda's mother cooked the chicken better than anybody in the whole village, and Kanda always looked forward to the chicken with its golden soup that displayed sparkling eyes. The irony of it all was that Kanda's mother did not eat chicken herself! People went to church in their finest clothes. Then the following day, Boxing Day, the kids as well as the adults would go out calling out *karimubokisi* (what's in the box) to other people with playful expectation of a gift of money, something similar to the American tradition of trick or treat at Halloween. It was all fun.

One of the most exciting expectations for kids at Christmas was getting new clothes. In addition to whatever their parents bought them, which was not always much, Kanda and his siblings always looked forward to new clothes from Auntie D. Auntie D worked as a nurse at a hospital in Bulawayo, Zimbabwe's second largest city. Each year at Christmas, Kanda, his brothers, sisters, and cousins on his mother's side received new clothes from Auntie D. Kanda and his siblings and cousins used to think that Auntie D was a very rich woman, unaware of the fact that each year, she labored for many hours on her sewing machine, making the clothes for her nephews and nieces. For Kanda, she would continue to play a crucial role in his upbringing, providing him with his first pair of shoes, his first set of dress pants and shirt and helping with school fees and his other financial needs in high school. For her, Kanda was the son she never had. Auntie D was a beautiful woman, pleasant, and a devoted Christian with a big heart for other people. It has never been clear to Kanda how and why such a person never got married. Auntie D lived and passed on without children of her own.

Some of Kanda's earliest and happiest memories as a little child are about his grandma's stories at the village fire. His grandfather had three wives. That way, Kanda had three grandmothers. The first wife and the second, who was Kanda's real grandmother, were rather old and kept much to themselves. It was the third and youngest that was the love of all the village children. Everybody called her *Mbuyanhini*; that is, *mbuya* or *ambuya* (grandmother) and *nhini*(young), translating to young grandmother. She was full of life and loved all the children. As the youngest wife, *Mbuyanhini* lived with Grandpa in his big round hut at the top end of the village. A few yards away in front of the big house was a rock surface, circular in shape, and bordered by a mango tree to the northwest. It was here that Grandpa, whose temper was known and feared far and wide, held his village court. It was also here that Kanda and the other village children gathered in the evenings to hear Grandma's stories.

Kanda remembers with nostalgia those evenings when the weather was clear and there was no pressure to sleep early because of school or work in the fields. Like all the other children in the village, he would quickly eat supper and rush to their meeting place with Grandma. The children would huddle around the fire to hear a new story. At times, his little sister would tag along, but he preferred to leave her behind as she would sometimes fall asleep and he would have to take her back home, causing him to miss some parts of an interesting story. There was always some jostling for vantage positions around the fire, either to sit closest to Grandma or to avoid where the wood smoke blew into your eyes. There would also be some shuffling, with lots of giggling, snickering, and even small fights, until Grandma clapped her hands, signaling she was ready. Even now many years later, Kanda can still smell the musty wood fire, feel the stinging sensation of wood smoke in his eyes, and hear the crackling sounds of the maize grains that Grandma would roast over the fire as a snack for the evening. In his mind, he can still see the dark African skies lit up with sparkling stars and hear the orchestra of night sounds from the crickets, owls, frogs, and other bush creatures. There would be the occasional scary moment, like when the children hear the hoo-wee cry of a hyena in the faraway mountain valley. This would be followed by lots of shifting and shoving among the children, especially those whose backs faced the bush, trying not to be pushed out of the security of the circle. Grandma would reassure them, reminding them of her favorite stories about the hyena being nothing more than a timid and cowardly scavenger.

Kanda and his friends never knew what story Grandma was going to tell. Some of the stories were new, but others would be old and well-known too. At times, she asked the children what story they wanted to hear, resulting in a deafening chorus of "Grandma this or Grandma that." The thing with Grandma, however, was that even with an old story, she would tell it with a new flavor that made it more interesting each time. Her stories always started with "Once upon a time." Kanda's favorite story was the one about the hare and the tortoise, and Grandma told it like this: "Once upon a time there was a hare and a tortoise. Hare always boasted about his cleverness and athletic prowess. He had won many contests in his life, but there were whispers among many fellow animals that he won most of the contests by picking only weak competitors. It so happened that one day, Hare challenged Tortoise to a race contest. Tortoise, always quiet, shy, and humble, was known to all to be a slow-moving animal. But it was an established animal custom to not turn down a challenge as this would be regarded as cowardly and demeaning. Word of the challenge reached the ears of the forest king, the Lion. As expected of him, the King sent messengers to all his subjects throughout the forest, inviting them to gather for the race. The race was to take place on a weekday when humans would be working in their fields so there would be no disruption from hunters. The standard contest was a two-mile race, starting from the huge msasa tree, a favorite of the King's, where he is usually seen relaxing under its cool shade, to the tall munhondo tree a mile away east and back.

"On the day of the race, all the animals of the forest were gathered around the msasa tree. There were all kinds of animals—big and small, four-legged, and two-legged. Eagle was sent upward to look out for humans and to report any approaching danger to those below. While many in the crowd felt that the race between Hare and Tortoise was uneven and unfair, the overall mood of the spectators was one of excitement and fanfare. The King finally called the two contestants to the starting line. The King's aide, Monkey, rattled the contest rules to all present and the specific instructions to the contestants. During all this time, Hare was busy strutting about, flexing his legs, and jerking his head and the big ears this way and that way, warming up for the race. Now and then, he would glance over at Tortoise with a smirk on his face. Tortoise simply walked to the starting line and waited. There was hushed silence when the King raised his paw. He then roared, 'Let the race begin. Go!' Hare and Tortoise took off amid a deafening explosion of cheers from the crowd." And of course, as all the children knew already, Tortoise won the race.

In the story of the hare and the tortoise, the hare always makes the same mistake. He takes off at high speed, and all you see is a cloud of dust as he disappears toward the munhondo tree. Somewhere, about halfway back, he decides to take a short rest, knowing it would take a long, long time before Tortoise catches up with him. Then he falls asleep. Meanwhile, tortoise slogs on quietly, reaches the munhondo tree, and passes Hare on the way back. By the time Hare wakes up with a startle, Tortoise is crawling across the finishing line to loud cheering from the crowd. Hare is jeered at as he follows behind, this time with his big ears flopping down in shame.

The end of the story was always received with jubilant cheers by the children. As with most of her stories, Grandma would review the story with the children. She would, for instance, ask them "Who would you rather be, Hare or Tortoise?" And they would all shout back in unison "Tortoise!" When asked why, some would say because Hare was too proud of himself or contemptuous of his opponent or that Tortoise was cool and focused or that they admired Tortoise for his humility and perseverance. Grandma would cap this up with some of her proverbs such as *kumhanya hakusi kusvika*, meaning that for one to succeed in life, it is not always speed alone that matters. The proverb in English goes, "Slow and steady wins the race."

Another favorite of Grandma's stories was of the hare and the baboon. Hare and his family invite Baboon and his family for dinner but stipulates that the guests' feet and hands must be clean when they come. Hare then burns the grass around his lair. When Baboon and his family arrive, their feet are smudged in soot, and they leave hungry. In turn, Baboon invites Hare and his family for dinner but does not stipulate any conditions. When Hare and his family arrive, they find that the dinner offered is high up a huge tree, and they return home hungry. Grandma would then explain the story that you do unto others as you would wish them to do unto you. Grandma used these stories to teach the children about some important values of life. She told many stories, where she would, in very interesting and relatable children's language, teach the importance of human values such as honesty, honor, integrity, ethics, respect, truthfulness, and reliability. And many of the stories Kanda and his age group remember about the great deeds of their ancestors were from Grandma at the village fire.

Grandma's influence extended beyond the evening gatherings. As Kanda and the other children outgrew Grandma's evening meetings, they continued to come to her for inspiration. For instance, at the end of each school term, the children were more excited to show their school reports to *Mbuyanhini* than to their own parents because she always had a special encouraging word for each child. When a child did well, she would praise him or her in a singsong fashion, reciting the child's totem and calling on his or her grandfathers and those before them to shower the child with more and more blessings. Whatever good day Kanda had, whether a successful day at hunting or fishing or a good game at school, it had to get to *Mbuyanhini* for acknowledgement and praise.

Mbuyanhini had only one child of her own, a son who grew up to earn the nickname Msande (the saint) among those around him because of his beloved and saintly nature. Like mother, like son, one might say. Msande has since joined the real saints beyond.

At the village, Kanda and the other children never had any ready-made toys. They made their own from all sorts of materials, such as clay, wood, wire, and pieces of cloth. Clay was the most common and readily available source for the toys, such as cars, houses, animals, kitchen utensils, dolls, and many others. Some of the clay toys were heated up to make them durable. Toy cars were the most popular among the boys. The older boys preferred cars made of wood, which would be big enough for them to actually ride on, complete with wheels, steering wheel, brakes, and even rearview mirrors. They would take the cars up on elevated ground such as an anthill and then drive down the slope. Very exciting, but there were lots of bad accidents too! The girls made dolls, complete with pretty little dresses, skirts, and blouses. Some of these village toys were so elaborate and finely modeled to a point of rivaling the ready-made toys from the city.

There was not a radio in the whole village, let alone television. Most of the children's recreation were outdoor games. The games were played mostly in the evenings, especially when the moon was out. The open area in front of the homesteads, extending the whole length of the village, was the playground. Among the most popular games were hide and seek, *chisveru, nhodo, pada, water* (no connection to actual water), and *mahumbwe.* The last one, *mahumbwe,* involved playacting the roles of adults as father and mother with their children. The girls used toy kitchen utensils to prepare the staple meal, using mud for *sadza* and leaves for vegetable relish. As the girls grew older, their parents would let them use actual kitchen utensils and real food ingredients, thereby transforming the make-believe childhood play into a real future role.

A major part of the children's outdoor recreation was singing and dancing, usually to the accompaniment of the drum. The children loved the singing and the dancing, and if one was especially good as a drummer, singer, or dancer, it earned them a special status in the village and even beyond. Occasionally, children from one village would go and join children in another village or hold informal singing and dancing competitions. For the older boys and girls, this interaction provided opportunities for meeting with others of the opposite sex and for courting.

Kanda enjoyed taking part in these village activities. He was very good at making toys, especially the wire and wood cars, and his were among the best. He also enjoyed the singing and dancing but was not particularly outstanding in either. Kanda was kind of reserved and somewhat shy, and looking back, some of his happiest moments were when he was doing his own thing alone or with Tobias.

Another source of recreation was the nearby Nhora River, great for swimming and fishing. Swimming usually took place during the dry season when the river was not at risk of flooding. Kanda and the other children were not taught to swim as such but learned to do so as a matter of course from constantly playing in the water. This started with the little boys and girls accompanying their mothers and older sisters doing laundry by the river, mostly during the weekends. As they grew older, the boys would separate themselves to the men's exclusive bathing and swimming spots along the river. All villagers knew which part of the river was for use by men and which by women, and for anyone to trespass to the other was taboo.

Kanda also liked fishing, not so much for the food but mostly for the act of fishing itself. At the time he learned to fish, modern fishing rods with reels and regular fishing hooks were not available. Even later, when hooks became available in the local stores, there was not any money to buy them. So for much of that time, Kanda and his cousins made their fishing hooks from chicken wire. They sharpened one end of the piece of wire, bent it into a hook, and secured it at the end of a string attached to a pole with a floater. For bait, they used worms, peanut butter, or *sadza*. The problem with the chicken wire hook was that it did not have an inner hook to secure in place either the bait or the catch, and unlike steel, the wire would easily unbend with the weight of a fish. Thus, it required some sort of acrobatic skill in order to successfully catch any fish, especially the big ones. One had to be really alert all the time, and the bobbing of the floater called for quick action! There was no leisurely reeling in of your catch because there would most likely be no fish at the end of the string by the time the hook left the water. The action called for was to yank the fish out, kind of surprising it before it could figure out what was going on. There were moments of disappointment when a big fish would unbend the hook and the fish fell back into the river. There were hilarious times too. Not knowing what to expect, the vigorous action to get the fish out was sometimes disproportionate to the size and weight of the fish, and a small fish would come out flying overhead to the riverbank behind. And if that fish became unhooked in the process, there would be much time spent looking for it in the brush. The situation changed over time, and Kanda has ever since remained hooked to the game of fishing.

Kanda was the first son of his family, and a lot was expected of him as he grew up. With the help of his father and cousins, he learned early to herd cattle, milk the cows, span the oxen, and to plough and weed the crop fields. Herding cattle was an onerous task. Each household was, in turn for a day or two, responsible for herding all the cattle of the village. This was ordinarily work for the boys, and it was an important phase in the development of young boys into tough young men. The grazing areas were communal, and boys and cattle from one village would mingle with others from nearby villages. This set the stage for many friendships as well as conflicts and fistfights among the boys. It was here that boys learned to fight and defend themselves. At times, the boys fought not because they had anything against one another. A lot of the fights were instigated by the older boys whereby even friends were matched for a fight. A common way to start a fight was that the older boys would build two mounds of dirt on the ground and say to one boy "This is your mother's breast" and then say the same to another boy for the other mound. One of these two boys would then be told to thrash the mound of the other, who would then feel insulted in front of all the other boys present. This never failed to start a fight. One of Kanda's many uncles at the village, Erick, was notorious for arranging these fights. His family did not have any cattle, but he was often at the grazing fields just for this purpose. Kanda did not like fighting. He was not the aggressive type and was considered timid, but he had his share of fights as he grew up. And as expected, he abided by the prevailing code that "What happens at the grazing fields stays at the grazing fields." While the boys' fathers had some idea of what was going on, their mothers never knew.

There were other hazards facing Kanda and the other boys herding cattle. The boys did not have raincoats to protect them from the rain. When there were signs of rain coming their way, they would dig out a certain small bush plant by its roots. They would then point the roots toward where the rain was coming from, chanting "Rain don't come here, rain go that way," with a motion indicating where the rain should go, away from them. When the rain stopped or changed direction, they believed their magic worked. When it did not, they weathered the rain as best they could, usually huddled under a small bush. Sheltering under big trees was discouraged as tree trunks were prone to lightning strikes.

Another problem that the boys faced was when they became too playful and distracted and the cattle strayed into someone's crop field or vegetable garden. The boys would usually get a beating for this, and at times, payment would be demanded from their parents for damage to the crops. When the cattle broke out of their pens at night, the boys were expected to go out and round them up, often in pitch darkness. All the while when herding cattle, Kanda and the other boys went about the bush, over all kinds of terrain, barefoot, at the risk of thorn pricks, snakebites, and other hazards. There was always the fear of snakes, but snakebites were very rare.

Herding cattle had its upside as well. It was not uncommon to come back home with a rabbit, a deer, or a couple of birds that one would have caught during the day. Like most people in the village, Kanda's family always had a dog or two. The dogs always accompanied the boys when they went out to herd cattle. Often, as the cattle moved through the bush, they would startle a rabbit or deer, and a chase would ensue. Or the boys would specifically go hunting in places where the animals were likely to be found. Every boy of Kanda's age group learned to shoot birds with catapults made of rubber from the inner tube of a motor vehicle tire, with a patch of leather to hold a small stone and a handle made of a stick with two branches spread out at an angle. They also learned to set traps for small animals, birds, and field mice.

Another upside for being out in the bush was the abundance of wild fruit. When out with the cattle, the boys were expected to return close to home around noon to get their lunch before heading back out for the rest of the day. When they did not show up, no one worried, knowing they were content helping themselves to the wild fruits. There were many kinds of fruit out there: *maroro, matamba, nhunguru, tsvanzva, tsomboribodo, hacha, mazhanje, hute, mabowu, matohwe, tsamviringa,* and many more. It's amazing that within a short span of a people's life, all these fruits are now just history, as the bush is decimated by man.

It has been said that "you can get the African out of the bush, but you cannot get the bush out of the African." While this has been said with a derogatory intent, it can be viewed in another way to be true about the attachment to nature one develops growing up in the countryside. An attachment that lives with you, even long after you have left the life in the bush. Kanda's earliest awareness of his world was the lush bush, the thick forests, the tall grass, and the mountains that extended far away into the horizon. Even the grey mud huts and their grass thatch blended perfectly with the rest of the natural surroundings. Pictured together with all the animals, the birds and other smaller creatures, the rivers and the fish; all under the clear blue African skies, with the sun, the moon, and the stars represented, in Kanda's mind, the blueprint from which God created the rest of the world. A world in which during his lone and quiet moments, Kanda wondered about the many marvels of creation. Even when in company of others, he would find himself wrapped up in his own private world, musing about the wonders of the world. Like when working in the crop fields with his family, he would find himself wondering about such things as the burying of the maize seed into the ground and, from the apparent decay, the sprouting of new life to support human life. His little mind was also fascinated by what he saw as the interdependence and interconnectedness of all living things. The cow feeds on the grass, and from the cow, man gets milk and meat, and in turn, human waste goes back to the ground to feed the grass. There were no toilets then, and people used the bush. He would get carried away by his imaginings, extending this chain of events to include inanimate things, such as the breakdown of bits and pieces of stone into sand, which, over time, become the soil that supports plant life. Kanda spent a lot of time in this private world of his, enjoying what he saw or trying to figure things out and often wondered if other people saw things the same way he did. For instance, when he and the other boys were busy chasing away the baboons and monkeys from the maize fields or were woken up to chase away hyenas from attacking cattle in the pens, he never regarded these animals with hostility, looking at the whole situation from the point of view of the general fight for survival among all creatures. He never saw any contradiction in, say, his love for the birds and their beauty and his hunting them for food. He would also ascribe human characteristics to other living things, wondering, for instance, whether cows, fish, birds, or even trees had some language of their own beyond human perception. He would marvel at how the small ant could travel long distances from its home and manage to find its way back with food or at birds' ability to build intricate nests from bits of grass or how wasps always seem to want to build their nests close to birds' nests, only to realize that it was in fact the birds that sought to build near the wasps for protection against humans and other predators. These musings would go on and on, and Kanda never thought them weird. He would get so lost in himself to the point of sometimes getting into trouble for being absent-minded. Other people would worry about his apparent loneliness when he was actually enjoying himself immensely.

Kanda views his growing up at the village one of his greatest life's blessings. It gave him the gift of nature. He and the other village kids often envied their cousins growing up in the city. But Kanda somewhat felt that none of the glitter and trinkets of the city could rival the joy from his intimacy with raw nature, like the experience of the smell of earth after a sudden downpour of rain. A child growing up devoid of the experience of that musky smell of cow dung permeating the morning mist as the sun rises must surely be missing something. Even the beauty of the stars is best seen in the dark of the countryside.

Kanda will always carry his childhood world vivid in his mind, but much has changed on the ground. The Chitenga mountain, once imposing and vibrant with abundant life, is now barren, reduced to a hideous mound and the once roaring Nhora River, now a blind meander, its life sapped by upstream dams and siltation. The forests too are gone, with many of the animals, the birds, and the wild fruit. No more happy children singing and dancing under the moonlight. The village children now have to join their city cousins to go to the zoo to see the baboon, in a cage. It's now crowded human settlements everywhere, both regular and squatter, with no open meadows to roam free, in contemplative quietude. Even the bogeyman has since shied away. The village drum is now mute, and the stars don't seem as bright anymore. Nowhere is the spiritually haunting mbira music heard. The remaining village people looking emaciated and spiritless. It's like a whole world shutting down. Kanda's people.

Florence at age twelve with grandma at the village (1966)

New family homestead at the village, rebuilt in 1985

Kanda's mother

Kanda's father

KANDA GOES TO SCHOOL

My child, never go west
Go east, north, south, to any end
But never to the west
For the woes of the land
Are born of the West

Kanda's father as well as Kanda's grandfather, Chitate, wanted the best for his future, but it was a different future each envisioned for him. Both father and grandfather were nationalists, but each of a different mold and perspective. Grandfather hated the white man for taking his land, pushing and confining him and his people to arid, sandy soils. He was bitter at the white man for imposing a limit on the size of his herd of cattle, his source of wealth and power, and, as if that was not enough, demanding payment of tax from the little left of him. He hated the missionaries for not only denigrating his religion, but worse still, for turning his people away from their traditional way of life. Their religion was an assault on his people's culture, their identity, and their link with their ancestors and their *Mwari*. Grandpa saw the white man's religion as a devious ploy to disguise and justify his greed and plunder. His views and feelings were in line with the often-told story that when the white man came, he handed the Bible to the people, and while they knelt down praying, with their eyes shut, heads bent, foreheads close to the ground, and their backsides up in the air, the white man rushed past them to grab the land behind them. When the people finally opened their eyes, their "Amen" sounded like an affirmation that "Yes, the deed is done, the land is indeed gone!" The people were left holding the Bible, and the white man got away with the land. In all this according to Grandpa, the white man was ultimately bent on destroying his people, both spiritually and literally.

As a result of his views about colonialism, Grandpa did not want anything to do with the white man. Because he wanted his children to grow up respecting and embracing his people's way of life, he saw education as one of the white man's weapons to frustrate and deny this from happening. Of any of his children who managed to get some education, it was their mothers who paid the fees from their own resources. He would not, as many fathers did, part with any of his many cattle to raise money for the fees.

Kanda's father was also a nationalist, with no less hatred for the white man, but he saw things differently from his own father. He had somehow reconciled himself to a distinction between the men of the cloth and the rest of the settlers who had come for selfish reasons. He embraced the former and declared the other an enemy of the people. He became a fervent preacher on the one hand, and on the other, a fiery opponent of colonial rule. He never saw any contradictions in these two roles. In fact, he regarded them as complementing each other, converging to enhance both the spiritual and social well-being of the people. And he saw education as another critical dimension in the overall effort to uplift the lives of the people and also as a weapon with which to fight the white man at his own game. He was also aware of his own shortcomings in dealing with the challenges of the new unfolding world and strongly believed that for his offspring to survive and thrive in the future, they needed education. He had a very strong desire for his children, both boys and girls, to go to school.

When Kanda's parents told him that he was going to go to school, he was very excited about it. The whole village would get to know about it. But the first person he wanted to tell was, of course, *Mbuyanhini*, and she was just as excited as he was. She told Kanda that one day soon he would become a great teacher like Mr. Zonde, a long-standing and well-respected teacher from the neighboring village to the north. *Mbuyanhini* could already see into the future, when Kanda would buy a car that would take her to the clinic when she got sick. It was all exciting talking to Grandma about school. All the while, Grandpa was nearby working on a wooden handle for his hoe and appearing totally uninterested in what Kanda and Grandma were talking about. When Kanda finally addressed him directly about the news of his going to school, all he got was some uncommitted grunt. At the time, Kanda had no idea about Grandpa's distrust of education, and he did not place any particular significance to his response. Grandpa did not have the easy, playful relationship that is usually expected of grandparents and their grandchildren. Kanda and the children were somewhat fascinated as well as afraid of him because of his temper. Grandpa had one of his arms, the left one, amputated below the elbow. There were many stories about how this came to be, but Kanda never knew to this day what the actual cause was. When he got angry, Grandpa would swear nonstop, wriggling the stub of this arm toward whoever upset him. Kanda and many of the other children had been at the receiving end of this fury while trying to sneak into his orchard to help themselves to the tempting ripe mangoes. He somehow always knew when the kids were going to try and do this. There was no doubt, however, that he loved all his grandchildren, and Kanda had no reason to believe that the reaction he got from him about him going to school was anything but his own strange way of expressing his approval.

The year was 1954, and Kanda was to start school that January. He was already nine years old, whereas the standard age to start school was seven. This standard was, however, not strictly adhered to as most of the children did not, at that time, have birth certificates. The most common method used to establish eligibility to start school at the time, in the rural areas at least, was to show if a child could place one arm over their head and be able to touch their ear on the other side of their head. If a child could do that, he or she was deemed old enough to start school, but if not, they would have to try again the following year. Although Kanda, like most of the other children, did not have a birth certificate, it was not this eligibility test that delayed his start at school, however. He had a baptismal certificate to confirm his age if that had been necessary. It had, however, been his parents' decision to wait until he was grown up enough to endure the long trip to Chindotwe School five kilometers away. Kanda had to go to Chindotwe, a Methodist Church school instead of the nearby Gorwa, a Salvation Army school. The school a child went to was determined by where the parents went to church. Kanda's parents were prominent members of the Methodist Church, and his father was a senior lay preacher of the church. In fact, Chindotwe church and school were founded by Kanda's father and Uncle Jack, Kanda's father's older half-brother. Kanda's father, a self-taught brick layer, built the original church building, which was, only recently in 2001, replaced by a larger one. The church and school would have been named after Kanda's family name instead of Chindotwe, but it was decided at the time to name it after the headman of the nearby village. As was the case with his older sisters before him, there was never any question as to which school Kanda would go to.

It had rained the night before Kanda's first day of school. Whenever it rained, there was always the question about which route to take to school, depending on whether Nhora River was passable or not. Kanda was still too young to take part in that decision, and so his sisters, Rebecca, half-sister from his father's earlier marriage, and Getrude would be making those decisions. When Nhora River was flooded, there were two alternate routes to take. The first of these was to heard north of the village, crossing Nhora River on a spot the villagers called *mangondo* (gorge), a place where the river flows through huge boulders. People crossed the river by jumping from rock to rock over chasms of churning waters below. After crossing the river, the route continued up north through a dense forest leading up to Chemhofu mountain before turning east to link up with the Nyava Road that passed by the school toward the Harare-Shamva road. Crossing the river at the gorge was very risky and dangerous, particularly for little children. This was especially so when the rocks were wet as there was the danger of slipping and falling onto the rocks and into the rushing water below. Kanda and his sister would not be using this route for a while until he was grown enough to take that risk. The other route entailed heading east of the village, through a low-lying grassy area that became swampy during the rainy season, toward the Harare-Shamva road, then follow the road over the Nhora Bridge, proceed for a while, before turning left onto the

Nyava Road to the school. Each of the alternative routes added an additional kilometer or so on the trip to Chindotwe School. On this day of Kanda's first trip to school, however, it had rained, but Nhora was barely passable due to not being in full flood. Kanda and his sisters managed to cross the river, with the water reaching knee level for little Kanda. There were no shoes to worry about as they were all barefoot. Kanda and his sisters proceeded up the riverbank, through the tall brush and the open plain, past Sika and Mavhunga villages to Chindotwe School.

The first major change that came with Kanda's going to school was that he would be registered and be known by his Christian name as given at his baptism, Timothy. The teachers always said the name correctly, but to most of the other children and people back home, he was Timoti. The name Kandashu was unknown to the school. With the passage of time, he began to dislike the African name, and any young child at the village who dared call him by that name soon learned that they would do so at their own peril.

Kanda does not recall any bullying or other unpleasant experiences during his first days at school. He was familiar with the school surroundings and knew many of his classmates from Sunday school. His family was well-known and respected by the teachers and the other children who knew them from church. His sisters, Rebecca and Getrude, were well regarded by the school and were often presented before the entire school during morning parade as a good example for the other children. They never missed school, were always punctual, attended Sunday school, were known to pray before going to bed, and were always smart. In this case, smart did not mean brainy but meant clean and presentable. The teachers always pointed out the contrast between Kanda's sisters (as well as Kanda himself in later years) who traveled the farthest distance to school through all kinds of hazards (rain, mud, dust, morning dew, etc.) and yet were able to be an example to other children, including those who lived closer to the school. Some children lived only a few yards away but had to be reprimanded for one thing or another, such as being late. It was with this family reputation that Kanda started his days at Chindotwe School. He did not fail the family cause, and for all the years that he was at Chindotwe, he was the only boy allowed to keep his hair growing because he was smart, while all the other boys were ordered to cut theirs short! As time would have it though, all that hair is now gone!

School always started with the morning inspection parade followed by a prayer. Then followed classroom work all morning and sports and other extracurricular activities in the afternoon. From the very beginning, there was an emphasis placed on arithmetic, English, and Bible study. The children learned the alphabet and studied handwriting as a subject. A lot of work was done in the sand to save on writing books and pencils, and the children used bundles of sticks to learn how to count. The afternoon activities were mainly athletics, soccer for the boys and net ball for the girls, and choir practice. On the days when only the older boys and girls stayed at school in the afternoon, Kanda would hang around the school waiting for his sisters as it was considered unsafe for him to go back home on his own. Kanda does not remember much about his own participation in sports but recalls being lumped up with the girls in the school choir.

Much of the four years that Kanda was at Chindotwe School is now just a blur, but a few incidents stand out in his memory. In Kanda's school days, primary school started in Substandard A, followed by Substandard B, then Standards 1, 2, onward to Standard 6. A child had to pass the end-of-year examination in order to proceed to the next level. At the end of Kanda's first year, his class teacher was said to have left the school without grading the class test papers or presenting whatever he had done with them to the school authorities. As a result, Kanda and his whole class were made to repeat Substandard A the following year! It has remained a mystery to Kanda why the school did not just give them another end-of-year examination.

The other thing Kanda remembers about his time at Chindotwe School was when one day, he and his sisters stayed at school for sports and their mother brought them lunch. His mother usually brought the lunch in a basket covered with a doily that was beautifully decorated with lace around the edges. Most of the time, her food smelled really good, even from a distance, attracting the attention of other hungry children nearby, which made Kanda feel very proud of his mother. The other children brought their own lunch or their parents did, and they would sit scattered about the school grounds in the open or under the shade of trees, depending on the weather. This day was like any of the other days, except that Kanda's mother had brought with her a different kind of lunch. It was not like something unusual that he had not had at home, but something that he really liked but had not had at school before. Inside the lunch basket was a big plate with food and another plate covering the food. On this day, the food was the regular staple *sadza* with field mice as the relish. As Kanda's mother lifted the plates out of the basket, there were tails poking out of the plates into the open in full view of everyone around! The shocked reaction from Kanda and his sisters, especially Kanda, was instantaneous, hushing their mother to put the plates back into the basket. Kanda hoped nobody saw what had happened. Knowing that any of the other children would have reacted the same way was of no comfort. The field mice were a delicacy, especially *shana*, not only to Kanda's family but to many in the country. However, this was not the kind of delicacy any child would want displayed in front of other children at school. It would be the talk of the day at school! So that day, Kanda and his sisters ate their lunch from inside the basket, enjoying their delicacy hidden from the view of the other children on the school grounds.

The other incident that Kanda remembers very clearly to this day involved a girl, the first of many such occurrences he would fortunately or unfortunately experience as he grew up. In Kanda's estimate, this girl was the most audacious of them all. Her name was Grace, and she was slightly younger than him. She was very beautiful, with light skin, which in itself at that time was considered the hallmark of beauty. Grace lived with relatives at a village close to the school and spent most of her school holidays with her parents in the city of Harare. She was a very confident and outgoing type of person. Her time in the city made her much wiser about the affairs of modern living than the other children, most of whom had never been to a town, let alone Harare, the big capital city. Grace was glamorous in her attire and demeanor. She had beautiful clothes and was one of only a few that wore shoes to school.

In contrast, Kanda was just the typical country boy who could only see life through a very constricted rural prism. He had never been to any town. In fact, he had never ridden a bus or car to go anywhere. The village and its surroundings were all the world he knew. He was reserved and kept much to himself. He was dogmatically religious with a very strong sense of what was right and what was wrong. He had a strict and provincial view of the accepted norms of behavior for boys and girls. Kanda does not recall having any interest in girls, and if he had, it would have been in a girl of the same outlook as his. At that time, it was unthinkable to Kanda and many others that a girl could propose love to a boy. For any girl who knew Kanda, to think of it and to actually go ahead and do so would be very daring. And that is exactly what happened!

Grace wrote a letter proposing her love to Kanda and gave it to Elias, Kanda's friend, to pass on. Kanda's reaction was explosive! He was enraged beyond words. He called her names and wanted to go ahead and beat her up! Elias, who had an easy and open-minded view of things, was surprised at Kanda's ferocious reaction to the letter. He intervened to save the lovelorn girl. As time passed, long after he left the school, Kanda felt embarrassed by the incident and felt genuinely sorry for the way he treated the beautiful young girl, whose only crime was to love him, to think him worthy of her love, and to have the courage to take the first step. Many years later, when Kanda was grown up and a little wiser about the affairs of girls, he made enquiries about Grace but never had the chance to see her again. Kanda would later serve as Elias's best man at his wedding in 1973, and Elias, in turn, would do the same for Kanda at his wedding years later.

The trip to and from school could be very challenging, especially during the rain and winter seasons and the very hot summer months. There were also, however, times of fun along the way. As Kanda and his sisters traveled the long distance to their Methodist school, there were also children from the Sika village who traveled the same distance on the same path in the opposite direction to their Salvation Army school at Gorwa. Both groups were in sympathy with each other for the long trips they made to school, and when

Nhora was in flood, each had to find alternative routes to school. Sometimes, they shared snacks when they met. As was common among neighboring villages, there were traces of blood or clannish relationships between the two groups. They thus had a fairly good relationship, but they also played tricks on each other. Both resented being the first on the route to beat the morning dew for the other on their shared path. What would happen was that the first group to reach the patch of dense grass by Nhora River would sacrifice by going deep into the tall grass away from the part of the path with the most dew so the that the other group would have to beat the dew for themselves as they went the other way. Another trick was to tie some grass across the path out of view close to the ground so that the other group would trip as they hurried past that area. Both groups were in the habit of hiding some snacks, usually roasted or boiled mealie (corn) cobs in the bush, to eat on the way back from school. When the snacks went missing, both groups weren't sure whether it was the other group responsible or other children herding cattle in the area. Both groups accused each other of dirty tricks but would at times laugh together about all this.

Kanda completed Standard 1, the highest grade at Chindotwe Primary School, at the end of 1957 and had to transfer to the Salvation Army Gorwa Primary School the following year. School was now only a kilometer away from home on a clear and safe road. Kanda was still adjusting to the new environment when during the August school holiday, after the second term, he had to leave Gorwa for another faraway school.

KANDA LEAVES THE VILLAGE

Uprooted from his birthplace
To the unfamiliar, up West
And what would Grandpa say
Should he have any sway

Kanda and his friends were up the huge fig tree, eating and collecting figs, when someone called from below that he was wanted at home. The boy sent for him had no idea why. Kanda sensed that it had to be something important as there were no chores that he was expected to complete that afternoon. It was the second Sunday afternoon of the August school holiday. Kanda rushed home with scratches all over his legs and arms from climbing trees. There was a surprise waiting for him at home. He wished he had known in advance so that he could have cleaned himself up before meeting his favorite *sekuru*, Uncle Dan, his mother's young brother. Uncle Dan was a very affectionate person with a hearty infectious laugh that worked his facial muscles up to partially hide his eyes. There was a radiating presence about him, and when he spoke, everyone around him listened. He was, at a relatively young age, a many-time winner as a school choir master.

The bigger surprise for Kanda was that his Uncle Dan had come to take him with him to KweKwe (then known as QueQue), a town about two hundred kilometers from Harare. Uncle Dan had been sent to get Kanda by his and Kanda's mother's older brother, Uncle James, who wanted Kanda to live with his family and attend school at the Globe and Phoenix Mine, where he was the headmaster. Kanda's family welcomed this development for him. His sister Getrude had already left to live with Uncle Kennedy and attend school in Shurugwi (then known as Selukwe). There were hasty preparations for his departure, and Kanda made his goodbyes that evening, which meant visiting every family in the village for their well wishes. He and Uncle Dan left the following morning. The trip was an exciting experience for Kanda, boarding a bus to Harare and then the train overnight to KweKwe.

KweKwe was a medium-size town in the Midlands Province in the center of the country, roughly halfway between Harare, the capital city to the northeast and Bulawayo, the second largest city to the southwest. KweKwe would come to have some special significance for Kanda. His future wife and the love of his life was only eight months old when he arrived in the town, and he would one day return to find her.

Conditions of living at the Globe and Phoenix Mine, as the case at the other mining compounds, had some characteristics of urban life—large and small buildings, electricity, running water, paved roads, shops, and so on. However, the way of life in the compounds was different from the openness of town or city life. The residents at the mine all worked for the one employer who controlled and influenced how they lived. It was a culture of subservience to the mine authorities, which constricted their view of the outer world. The situation was compounded by the fact that many of the workers at the mine were immigrants, mostly from Malawi, who were regarded as submissive by nature, resulting in a culture often referred to, in a demeaning way, as compound mentality. The situation at the Globe and Phoenix Mine, however, differed slightly from that of other mine compounds in that it was within short distance from the KweKwe town proper, where people could walk to and from to shop, attend other activities, and mingle with the town folk.

Uncle James lived with his wife, his older brother's son, Aggrey, and his wife's niece, Margaret. The latter two were slightly younger than Kanda. Uncle James also took care of another older boy who was not a relative. He and his wife had no children of their own. Kanda settled in with his new family in the big house in the better part of the compound reserved for the elite society at the mine. He now walked only a few yards to and from the school, enjoying the special status of being the nephew of the headmaster of the school.

There was breakfast of tea and buttered bread, some meat with lunch and dinner, and running water for bathing and laundry. There were no more cattle to herd nor the hard work of ploughing, weeding, and harvesting in the fields. All that was expected of Kanda was to study, and there were more books at home and school than he could ever need to feed his hunger for education. Although he was not living the proper city life, did not yet have beautiful clothes, and still went about barefoot, his new life was a far cry from that at the village. He missed his family and friends at the village though, often imagining with nostalgia his friends going about the things he used to enjoy with them. Kanda's life in KweKwe was short-lived and at the end of his first school term in December 1958, he had to leave for another life.

KANDA ON THE FARM

Back to the land
With its joys and chores
The brief urban glimpse
An unkind, tantalizing tease

At the end of the school year 1958, Uncle James was transferred to Senga Primary School in Senga African Township of Gweru City (then known as Gwelo), which was about sixty kilometers southwest of KweKwe. In colonial Rhodesia, people of different races lived separately by law. In the towns and cities, the white people and the colored (term used to describe those of mixed races) lived in what was referred to as suburbs, which were separate from the residential areas for the Africans, referred to as African townships. There were strict rules of residency in the townships as a means of maintaining law and order among the urban Africans. The township houses belonged to the local authorities, who then rented them out. One had to be lawfully registered to stay in a township and could only live with members of one's immediate family. Kanda could, therefore, not live with his uncle's family in Senga Township, but Aggrey was able to do so as their son because of the shared family name. It was then decided that instead of sending Kanda back to the village, he would go and live with his mother's oldest brother, Munyuki, who owned a farm at Waze, in the Musengezi Small Scale Purchase Area for small scale African farmers. This was near Chegutu Town (then known as Hartley), about halfway between KweKwe and Harare. Kanda would continue with his schooling there at nearby Waze Primary School.

Life on the farm was a throwback to his life at the village and much worse in some respects, especially after the brief promise of a life without toil in town. Farm life meant hard work. At the village, as in communal reserves generally, farming was for subsistence purposes only, with long periods of rest, especially during the time from harvest to the next cropping season. Kanda found living on the farm a completely different kind of life. There was work of one kind or other throughout the year, ploughing, seeding, weeding, harvesting, winter ploughing in preparation for next cropping season, raising chicken, picking fruit for the market, and the list went on. Like most other small-scale farmers, Kanda's uncle did not have hired labor, relying entirely on the family members for the farm work. At the age of fourteen, Kanda was one of two boys at the farm old enough to shoulder much of the hard man's work. During the busiest times, this entailed waking up at dawn to do some work in the fields and then return to the house to prepare to go to school.

Another downside of farm life is the isolation from other people. Apart from the time at school, it was difficult to meet and make friends because the homesteads were far apart from each other.

There was a major consolation though to all this. Musengezi was the home of the Manyikas, Kanda's mother's people, and he was dearly loved and had a special place among them. About five kilometers west of Waze, at Dombwe, was the farm of Dick Manyika, his maternal grandfather. Kanda was the first son of Dick's first daughter. Traditionally, that is a special position in the maternal family known as *chigadzanhaka*, meaning the one who oversees the inheritance of the wives of the uncles when the uncles die. And a common joke is that a cunning *chigadzanhaka* can end up as *chigaranhaka* (the one who inherits) by appropriating the uncle's widows for himself instead! The arbitrator becoming the sole beneficiary of his own arbitration!

Dick Manyika's family was a large family of two wives, Marutenga, the first, and Kadede, the second, and thirteen children. Kanda's account of the children, starting with Marutenga's children, in order of seniority is as follows:

Munyuki. Firstborn. Former policeman turned farmer and owner of farm at Waze. Traditional historian and philosopher. Religious leader. Large family with eleven children. Obtained driver's license at age seventy.

James. Teacher and pioneering black headmaster. Got Kanda from the village to KweKwe. Strong advocate for education. Senator in Zimbabwe's legislature at independence.

Agnes. Kanda's mother. The best mother and best cook ever!

Kennedy. Teacher and headmaster. Got Kanda's elder sister Getrude to live and attend school with his family. Zimbabwe's ambassador to Yugoslavia. SADC Special Envoy on the DRC crisis. SADC Special Envoy to Namibia. Author of *Beyond My Dreams.*

Deliwe. Auntie D. Big heart and a definition of love. You know somebody loves you when they invest in you with no guarantee or expectation of a return on the investment.

Daniel. Uncle Dan. Last born. Came for Kanda at the village. Teacher and multiple award-winning school choir master. Diplomat to USA and Ethiopia. Affable with irresistible charm. Women loved him to bits!

Kadede's children are as follows:

Robson. Firstborn. A political hothead. Commander of the Zambia camp for Zimbabwe liberation war fighters. First deputy minister of Labor and Social Welfare at independence.

Issac. Teacher, headmaster, and farmer. Kanda's schoolmate at Tegwani Institute where he was training as a teacher.

Cleopas. Slightly older than Kanda and also living at Waze farm with Kanda. Self-appointed family diplomat. Labor relations officer.

Tandiwe. Pure heart, tender, and loving aunt.

Wellington. Younger than Kanda. Long-standing employee of Zimbabwe Alloys. Farmer and polygamist. Like father, like son.

Viola. Loving aunt, married to an engineer, and entrepreneur.

Edward. Last born of the family. Long distance trucker. Passed on young.

Dick's wives were related and regarded as sisters. As a result, the closeness and harmony among the wives and the children was more than is common in polygamous families. The overall family atmosphere was such that Kanda was blind to any distinctions between the two sides of the family.

He loved and was loved by all his uncles, aunts, and their children. At special occasions, such as holidays, weddings, and funerals, he would have the opportunity to meet with most of them. They were almost all an outgoing and gregarious people. At family gatherings, they would display their common gift of song, singing with such rare beauty and harmony for such a large group of people, a gift passed on to some of Kanda's siblings but not to him!

It was here at the grandparents' farm that Kanda spent most of his time when free from work on the farm at Waze. The two grandmothers pampered him, competing to spoil him with special food treats that they reserved and then gave to him behind half-closed doors when the other children were playing outside. His grandfather was somewhat aloof but showed his affection by calling or referring to Kanda by his clan name, *Chikwaka*, which he pronounced *Chikwakwa*! Like Grandpa Chitate, he also had a large mango and guava orchard, which he was very protective of.

From the time he left the village, Kanda's life became closely intertwined with that of his mother's people. He was home away from home. Even today, some of the people from the Musengezi farming area call him by his mother's family name. And one of his father's brothers always says whatever Kanda's life achievements are, they are attributable to his maternal family.

Kanda completed his Standard 3, the highest level at Waze Primary School, at the end of 1959. He does not remember much of note at the school that year. Uncle Munyuki and Kanda's father arranged that he would now go to a nearby boarding school, Marshall Hartley Mission School, which was run by the Methodist Church mission.

In the meantime, he would see his family at the village for the first time in over a year.

Uncle Munyuki

Uncle James

Uncle Kennedy

Auntie D

Uncle Dan

Uncle Robson

KANDA RETURNS
TO THE VILLAGE

To truly realize your love for home and family
Be gone awhile

Just before he left for the village, Kanda received a Christmas present, which turned out to be one of his most memorable Christmas gifts ever. Kanda and his cousins expected that there might be some Christmas presents from Auntie D as always. Among the presents that came was a special package for Kanda containing a pair of black shoes, a white dress shirt, and a pair of khaki shorts. The shoes and the dress shirt were way beyond Kanda's expectation. It was an emotional moment for Kanda that he would now get to wear shoes and smart clothes. Having left the village in near tatters, he was now going back home a transformed person. The combination of the gift of clothes, Kanda's going to spend Christmas with his family, and him going to boarding school in the New Year marked a high point in Kanda's life.

Kanda was going to spend two weeks at the village and would return to the farm from where he and Uncle Cleopas, who was also going to boarding school for the first time, would leave for Marshall Hartley Mission School. Arrangements were made that his father would meet him at the train station in Harare. Kanda's first trip to Harare from the village had been a blur, a rush from the bus station to the train station. This time, however, he got to see a bit of the city. His father met him at the train station early Saturday morning. Together they walked through town to the main post office, where his father was working as a driver. From there, they walked to Amato shopping center on Kingsway Street, where Kanda was left in the care of a cousin named Francis. Francis was working as an attendant in a shoe shop at Amato. Kanda had known his older cousin as they grew up, but Francis had changed dramatically from the village boy Kanda knew to the well-groomed city young man he now was. The fact that he wore sunglasses and a straw hat in the store did not seem odd to Kanda but instead added to the appearance of urban sophistication. Francis was mostly busy with customers and did not pay much attention to Kanda. It was a real treat when he bought Kanda some fish and chips and a bottle of Fanta. The store was very busy, serving mostly Africans, with a few colored and white people from time to time. Francis appeared to enjoy serving and chatting with them all. Kanda enjoyed the goings-on and did not notice how quickly time passed by. Just after lunchtime, his father came to take him to the bus for home. His father was not himself going to the village that weekend. He bought Kanda some groceries to take home. The bus arrived at the village bus stop just before sunset.

There were some people on the bus also going to Kanda's village, relatives of one kind or other. It took some of them a while to recognize him, and they all said how grown he was. On disembarking from the bus, Kanda kept company with the other villagers through the thick brush in Mutatu farm up to the edge of the farm where the bushes gave way to a wide clearing that marked the beginning of the native reserve and Kanda's village below. Kanda stepped back and let the other people proceed. He needed some time to himself to absorb the view before him. To truly realize your love for home and family, be gone away awhile. It was like Kanda was seeing this place, truly seeing it all, for the very first time. He was born here, and he grew up here, but it seemed like he had never, as it were, had the opportunity to set himself aside so he could have a full view of his habitat. The imposing Chitenga Mountain to the southwest, the golden sun to the left, coursing slowly through the clouds to the horizon, and the picturesque village below was a view that would last forever in Kanda's memory. Though Saturday afternoon was normally a time to leave the crop fields to rest, Kanda could see some dotted figures here and there of people still working in the fields. The smoke spiraling up from several of the village huts brought forth strong feelings of nostalgia. Kanda could hear the bark of a dog or two and the crowing of a roaster. He had indeed arrived back home.

News of Kanda's arrival reached the village before he did. His younger siblings came rushing to meet him halfway. They could not help gaping at him, their brother in such smart clothes and shoes! Little did they notice how uncomfortable he was beginning to feel in his new shoes. His reception by the family and the whole village was overwhelming. His siblings' excitement and mother's pride showing all over her face was very touching. But before Kanda could settle down and take it all in, he had to perform a ritual that would become part of his routine whenever in the future he returned or left the village. He would go and pay his respects to Grandpa Chitate and all the grandmothers. And of course, Mbuyanini was the most exciting encounter of them all. He would also go up and down the village, greeting his uncles, aunts, and everybody else. By the time he returned to his family homestead, Kanda was really exhausted. The overnight train trip from Chegutu to Harare, the long stay in the city, the bus ride to the village, and all the excitement of his arrival home had taken a toll on him. He was glad to finally take off his shoes, which were now pinching his feet. The family enjoyed the special meal of rice and chicken that his mother had prepared for the occasion.

The following day, Sunday, the family did not go to church in order to allow Kanda time to rest. Kanda used the time to catch up with his cousins and friends. The family did go to church the following Sunday, and everybody there commented on how Kanda had changed and grown. His former schoolmates admired his fine clothes. The two weeks at the village passed by too quickly for Kanda, with lots of work in the crop fields and much time to play in the evenings and at weekends.

KANDA GOES TO BOARDING SCHOOL

A village child goes to school
Never for himself alone
But for the village as a whole

Soon it was time for Kanda to leave. He went up and down the village, making his farewells. As he went about, he received blessings and an assortment of gifts for the trip and to take to boarding school: a tickey here, a tin of peanut butter, some roasted peanuts, dry corn, and more even from some people he never knew had any interest in him. Kanda took the bus to Harare with his father, who then put him on the train for Chegutu.

At the farm, Kanda and Cleopas made their preparations and left for Marshall Hartley Mission. For Kanda, this was a huge and very exciting adventure. He and Cleopas put their suitcases on a bicycle carrier and walked the eight or so miles to the school.

Methodist missionary schools were not rich institutions. The general living conditions at the school were very basic, not much different from the general conditions in the surrounding rural area. For instance, there was no running water, and water was drawn from wells. People used pit latrines, and the floors in the students' dormitories were hard-beaten earth, which were then polished by applying cow dung every weekend. The students, both boys and girls, were responsible for polishing their own dorm floors with the cow dung, which caused a lot of consternation among the boys. In the villages, the polishing of the earthen floors with cow dung was done by the women. No men at their homes would ever be seen performing this chore, and yet now the boys faced this dilemma.

So what the boys resorted to doing was to wake up to go and collect their cow dung from the cattle pen very early, way before the girls were expected to come to the pen. If the boys overslept and were seen by the girls at the cattle pen, it would be the talk of the week! It was common knowledge that the boys did this chore the same way as the girls, but for any boy to actually be seen collecting the cow dung or to be known to be the one doing so at a particular time was scandalous.

The students slept on mats on the floor. They went to school without shoes, which they would only wear on Sundays and at other special occasions. Meals were mostly porridge for breakfast and *sadza* with vegetables or beans for lunch and dinner.

Kanda's memory of his days at this school has become blurred, but there are a few incidents he still remembers. During the three years at the school, he grew much taller and gained a lot of weight. People said it was the beans! He and a friend, Ticha, from the nearby Zvimba Native Reserve, were very close. Ticha had beautiful wavy hair with a hint of multiracial background, and at school, Kanda was the only one who cut his hair. One school holiday, Kanda and Ticha's parents bought them separately identical khaki shorts and shirts. The clothes were made of a finer khaki material referred to as sanforized and were exactly the same except for the sizes. Kanda was plump, and Ticha was slim.

There was also another girl incident at Marshall Hartley. There was this girl named Gift. Petit with light chocolate skin and beautiful black hair. She was the most beautiful girl in the whole school, confident, and very outgoing. She came from a well-to-do family in Bulawayo and traveled first-class on the train to school. She was one of few students who wore shoes to school every day. Looking back, Kanda does not believe that he, with his shy and provincial persona at the time, was the one who initiated the love relationship with Gift. It had to have been her who chose him instead! People used to say Kanda was very handsome back then though and smart too, meaning always clean and presentable. Kanda and Gift became boyfriend and girlfriend, but there was not much in the relationship apart from sending each other love notes and holding hands when on school outings, away from the eyes of the teachers.

On Saturday evenings, the school organized what was referred to as functions, a variety of entertainment activities in the school hall. On one such evening, Gift and a group of other girls were to take part in a drama in which she and another girl would perform the roles of males. Gift asked for Kanda's and Ticha's sanforized shorts and shirts. That evening, Gift put on Ticha's slim clothes, and the other girl, a little plump, put on Kanda's, and that set Kanda off pretty bad, angry that his girlfriend chose to put on Ticha's clothes and not his! How dare she! Jealousy, the sweet agony of teen love. Of course, it was all within himself alone, and Gift never knew.

One school term, Gift was a no-show at the school. She did not contact Kanda, and her friends seemed not to know anything about her absence as well. Kanda and Gift have not seen or heard from each other ever since. Kanda and Ticha have also not seen each other since. An attempt to reconnect with him years later ended with just a short phone conversation. After Marshall Hartley, Ticha joined the police force, where he remained until his retirement as a district police chief.

Kanda completed his Standard Six with satisfactory results and was now headed to another boarding school.

For the three years Kanda was at Marshall Hartley, he did not visit his family at the village. He spent his school holidays alternating between his uncle's farm at Waze and his grandparent's farm at Dombwe. During his time at Dombwe, he spent a lot of time with another uncle, Robson, a firebrand nationalist politician. Though generally a very nice person, he was considered a hothead with a very short temper. Each morning, Robson would cycle to the nearby business center to get the daily newspaper. While he attended to some chores at the farm, he would ask Kanda to read aloud for him the political news stories in the paper. The news articles were in English, and Kanda was only beginning to develop a grasp of the language. Uncle Robson did not have much patience with Kanda whenever he faltered in his reading. Being with him was an exciting as well as frightening time. Although Kanda grew up with a father who was a politician, it was really Uncle Robson who provided the foundation of his political consciousness. Uncle Robson eventually fled the country and ended up as camp commander of the gorilla freedom fighters in neighboring Zambia. He became the deputy minister of Labor and Social Welfare at Zimbabwe's independence in 1980.

KANDA GOES TO
HIGH SCHOOL

Kanda goes further West
What would Grandpa say
Should he have the say

Kanda did not formerly apply for admission to Marshall Hartley School nor to Tegwani Institute, where he was now headed. His place at Marshall Hartley was arranged by his Uncle Munyuki. To secure his place at Tegwani, his father took the train from Harare to Plumtree and walked the eight miles to and from the mission school to see the principal in person about his son's admission. At that time, he was using a walking stick because of a chronic leg problem. That's how important it was to ensure that Kanda went to high school. And not just any high school but the renowned Methodist Mission School, Tegwani.

Kanda was granted a form 1 place to start January 1963. Upon completion of his studies at Marshall Hartley, Kanda said his good-byes to his maternal people at Waze and Dombwe farms and returned to the village to prepare for his journey to the new school. Kanda's father had difficulty maintaining regular employment because of his bad leg. At this time, the family was surviving on market gardening and the sale of other produce from the surrounding farms at markets in the city. Thus, when Kanda was ready to start at his new school, there was not enough money to pay the school fees. This was going to be the pattern of things for the whole time he would be at Tegwani. The fees for Kanda at Marshall Hartley were not much and were shared between his uncle and his father, but this time, the fees were the sole responsibility of his father alone. Kanda did not carry any fees to school. The money was always sent by mail as it became available. Each time before Kanda left for school, the family prayed that they would be able to come up with enough money for the fees. Kanda will never forget one embarrassing moment at the train station in the presence of some of his schoolmates when his father pulled out a two shillings and six pence coin and gave it to him and said, "You know what the situation is at home, and this is all I have for you." Two and a half shillings when some of his schoolmates were boasting of pocket money of as much as five pounds and traveling second and third class on the train when Kanda was always traveling fourth class.

Tegwani Institute is in the Plumtree District, southwest of Harare and about 110 kilometers from the city of Bulawayo, 540 kilometers from Harare and almost 600 kilometers from Kanda's village. It is near the border with Botswana. Plumtree area is an arid, semi-desert place. Tegwani Mission shared a border with Nata Native Reserve, the land of the Kalanga people. Tegwani was a coeducational institution comprising a secondary school and a teacher training wing. Life at Tegwani was a huge improvement from the conditions at Marshall Hartley. There was electricity and running water with shower facilities. The dormitories were spacious, and students slept on beds. Breakfast was tea and bread, and lunch and dinner were *sadza* with vegetables, beans, and beef. There was a hall for student recreational activities and a tuck shop, which served the students with small items, including stationery and groceries. There was a variety of sporting and other social activities at the school.

One major change for Kanda was that most of his teachers and the principal, Mr. Hoskins, were Europeans (all white people were referred to as European), and all the lessons would now be taught in English. The education system in Rhodesia was segregated apartheid style. The white, the colored, and the indigenous African people had separate schools. The allocation of resources also followed that hierarchy, with the African schools being the least resourced. The African public schools in rural areas were run by African teachers. Likewise, in the urban African schools, the teachers were mostly African but with white headmasters. There was some difference with the African missionary schools, where some of the white missionaries were part of the teaching staff. Generally, the conditions of the African schools, whether rural or urban or missionary or government-run, were not as good as the white and colored schools. The rural ones were much worse. Among the missionary schools, the Catholic ones tended to have more and better facilities than the Methodists, Anglicans, Salvation Army, and the other church schools.

Up to this point, all of Kanda's studies, including English language, had been taught by African teachers. The only white person he had been close to was the LDO (the government land development officer), who used to visit the cattle dip tank and agricultural shows for the peasant farmers and would sometimes visit the village people in their crop fields. Even then, Kanda had no direct personal interaction with him. Also, the LDO mostly communicated with the villagers in *Chiraparapa* or *Silapalapa,* a bastardized language that was a mixture of English and the vernacular languages.

The new white teachers at Tegwani did not appear to have any difficulty understanding the students. While Kanda was quite good with written English, he and a few other students took a while to fully understand the teachers when speaking. Also, the white teachers pronounced his name differently, with the *o* in Timothy being silent.

Tegwani is where Kanda came out of his shell. He blossomed. Depending on the people around him, he would be either comical and clownish here or the serous and studious self. One significant thing that happened for Kanda was that he met a young man named Robert, who would become his best friend for life. On his first day in class, he shared a desk with Robert, from Epworth Mission, just outside of the city of Harare. Robert was unassuming but could be very funny. There was not much in common in their backgrounds. Kanda was rural, and Robert was urban, with a hint of sophistication associated with city life. Robert owned and played a guitar. He was not much of a singer, but he liked to sing anyway. Over time, there were other people who became part of their orbit. There was Calvin, a mathematics wizard who also owned and played the guitar. Maxwell was affable and funny to be around. Kanda believes that had Robert grown up in a country that valued performance arts, he would have done very well for himself. He would probably be a millionaire in America! He formed a music band with him on the lead guitar, Calvin on bass, and Kanda as the lead singer. Several times, they performed before the other students during the Saturday entertainment evenings. Their favorite song was "Hang on Sloopy" by the McCoys. The climax of the performance was where the song went instrumental and the lead singer would do a little dance and some shaking of body and head, resulting in his cap falling off his head to the floor. That never failed to raise an applause from the audience. Robert, Kanda, and the other friends also spent a lot of fun time at the Tegwani River trying to recreate *Superman*. Robert's idea was to produce a superman comic book. The tricky part was to create and capture superman in flight. Using the bedsheets, which they brought with them, one of them would go up the high riverbank and, using the bedsheets for wings, fly down to the sandy riverbed below, with someone with a camera taking a picture of the flight from the riverbank to the riverbed! The fall from the riverbank to the ground was just a blur, too swift to capture a clear picture. All they got from this action was sore tummies from lending on the dry riverbed.

This group of Kanda's friends also had a connection with Abraham, another chubby and affable young man. Kanda can't remember how the connection with him came about, but he and Abraham later found out that Kanda's sister Getrude and Abraham's father knew each other in the city of Bulawayo. Later on, during their years at Tegwani, in an incident mirroring the Ticha/Kanda sanforized khakis at Marshall Hartley Mission, Abraham's father and Kanda's sister bought Abraham and Kanda identical suits from the same Indian shop in Bulawayo! Whenever the two of them put on their suits together, there was always some kind of jealous resentment from the rest of the group. Nothing serious but something like "Oh, you old-fashioned guys keep to yourselves."

Kanda had two other friends, Edmund and Misheck, who were not connected to the other group of friends. The three of them were in the same house, Hlabangana, with yellow colors. There were three other school houses, Carter, Khumalo, and Aggrey. Edmund and

Misheck were a two-man bugle band that accompanied the boys' march from their dormitories to the morning church service every Monday to Friday. Now and then, Kanda would insert himself in the band to avoid the marching.

Kanda built many other loose personal associations based on various other interests such as Christian fellowship, sports, and politics. He had a friend called Danger who was trying to teach him the local Kalanga language. Kanda had several flirtatious relationships but nothing serious to talk about. Girls thought him handsome and liked him, but none captured his heart the way Gift had at Marshall Hartley.

Kanda approached his school work seriously, fully appreciative of the privilege to go to high school. In the country at the time, only a small number of about twelve percent of students who passed their Standard Six were able to proceed to secondary school, and many who qualified did not go because they could not afford the fees. Kanda was also aware of the tremendous sacrifice his family was making for him to further his education. He had assured them that he would do his best and wrote home regularly to update them on his progress.

Kanda's favorite subject was English, and he struggled with mathematics. For his junior certificate at the end of the first year in 1964, he passed with distinctions in the English language, arithmetic, general science, geography, history, and Latin and a credit in Bible knowledge and a pass in mathematics. He was top of his class that year. His family, especially his father, was ecstatic about his school performance.

Things began to change during his third and fourth year. The science studies were now more comprehensive with biology, physics, and chemistry now treated separately. Kanda had difficulty with the latter two and continued to struggle with mathematics. He continued to work as hard as before, but much of his time was now being taken up by many other interests in the school.

In his final years, Kanda probably had the most extracurricular positions in the whole school. He was a school prefect, house prefect, and secretary of the prefects' council. He was in the school athletic team, specializing in hop-step-and-jump and the sprints. He was the goalkeeper for his house soccer team. He was on the entertainments committee tasked with organizing entertainment activities for the students on Saturday evenings. He was a shop assistant working with one of the teachers' wives in the school tuck shop after school and on Saturday mornings. Kanda was on the committee of the Christian youth fellowship group, which met on Sunday afternoons for Bible study. He remembers clearly the Jim Reeves songs they used to play in those meetings. Kanda was also the founder and secretary of the Tegwani cultural club, which had AB, his history teacher, as its patron.

In his third year, Kanda and a few other young men were accepted on a two-year London preachers' course, which was conducted by the school chaplain, Reverend Canaan Banana. Reverend Banana would later become the first head of state for Zimbabwe at independence in 1980. The preachers' course entailed Bible study as well as practical preaching practice in the field. There were times when, on a Sunday afternoon, while other students were relaxing or studying, Kanda would be seen on a bicycle, Bible and hymn-book on the carrier, on his way to nearby Nata Reserve to deliver a sermon. He preached under the supervision of church elders at the congregations that he visited. He would preach in English, and someone at the church would translate to local languages. Kanda will never forget an incident when, in the heat of the moment, he abandoned English and spoke a few sentences directly to the congregation in their own language, and the audience was surprised and aroused, with lots of nodding and amens. The incident had the feel of a preacher briefly possessed by the Holy Ghost! One Sunday evening at the school, the trainee preachers were given a sermon to deliver to their fellow students and staff. This was the first time for the students to hear other students preach to them, and the sermon was very well-received. Some of the students said that the church service had had a greater impact on them than any other before from the regular adult preachers.

At the end of the course, Kanda and the other trainees were awarded provisional preachers' certificates, which allowed them to preach under supervision until they were fully certified to preach independently.

In his final year of school, Kanda was inducted into the Chaminuka Secret Society, an underground political group of students who met under a huge dry tree they named Chaminuka on the dry banks of the Tegwani River, way beyond the boundary of the school property. The group met regularly to share information on the political events in the country. The group shared information with a counterpart organization at Fletcher, a government secondary school in the city of Gweru. From time to time, the group also received information from outside the country in Zambia, where the Zimbabwe liberation forces were operating from. Kanda has retained a friendship since with one of the secret society members.

For the first three years at Tegwani, Kanda had not known anything about the secret political organization. He had, however, during that time, developed much interest in politics and the general political activities at the school. Unaware of the influence of this underground organization, he was one of a group of students who organized a demonstration against the colonial government in 1965 over its declaration of unilateral independence (UDI) from the colonial power, Britain. Rhodesia was then under the apartheid-style government of the Ian Smith regime. The regime had been in protracted negotiations with the British who were interested in a political settlement that would accommodate the indigenous African people in the governing of the country, leading toward eventual emancipation of the oppressed local population. No agreement could be reached, and the Smith regime decided to take the matter into their own hands by declaring Rhodesia independent from Britain on November 11, 1965.

Kanda was very active in the organization of the demonstration and was given the responsibility over the alarm clock so that he would be the one to wake up people for the start of the demonstration. The plan was that only the boys from form two to form four would take part in the demonstration, leaving behind the form ones and all the girls. On the appointed day, the boys would go to bed early. The alarm would go off at midnight, and Kanda would alert people to wake up. The staff, the form ones, and the girls were not supposed to know about the plan. The boys woke up, stealthily made their way from the dormitories, and met just outside the schoolyard on the road to Plumtree town some eight miles away. The plan was to march to the Native District Commissioner's office, demonstrate outside the office, and march back to school in time for the morning classes. The school somehow got wind of what was going on, and some of the staff followed and caught up with the boys a short distance away. They tried to persuade the boys to turn back to the school. The boys would stop and listen quietly. When the staff finished talking, they would clap their hands, disappear into the bush on both sides of the road, regroup further down the road, and continue. This was spontaneous behavior by the boys without prior planning. This was repeated several times, and then suddenly, there appeared two big police trucks from the opposite direction. Somebody had alerted the police in Plumtree.

The Rhodesian police were well-known to be brutal and were feared throughout the country. The boys knew it was no longer time for the hide and seek game they had been playing with their school staff. As the police arrived, the boys left the road and gathered on the sides of the road. When the police asked what the boys were up to, nobody answered for a while. When they repeated the question, someone in the group shouted that they wanted to get to the district commissioner. After conferring among themselves, the police ordered the students to get onto the trucks. When the boys just stood there without responding, the police fired a gunshot in the air. The gunshot sounded very loud and frightening, and each boy felt like they had been hit in the gut! For most of them, it was their first time to hear the sound of a gun. There was suddenly a scramble to board the trucks.

The police drove the boys to Plumtree with the school staff in tow. The boys were disembarked and sat on the grounds outside the District Commissioner's office. The police folded their hands and waited for the boys to say something. The students' plot had been disrupted by the arrival of the police. The idea had been to get to the District Commissioner's office, demonstrate outside, make some noises to protest the UDI, and then return to school in time for their morning classes. Thus, there was no petition or designated speakers. After a long silence, one boy stood up and gave a brief statement that the students were protesting UDI, and he sat down. When no one else spoke, the police said that if that was all they had to say, they could leave and get back to school. The boys were relieved because they had expected the worst to happen to them. Even then, it was not clear if that was the end of the story.

The return to school was a trot most of the way. The school staff accompanied them part of the way before they proceeded ahead. The boys got back to school in time for their showers, breakfast, and morning classes. As they arrived, the form one boys and the girls all gaped at them in surprise and awe. There was one form four boy who later became a prominent businessman who had not joined the march, and he was ridiculed as a coward and a traitor. There was some suspicion that he might have been the one who alerted the school staff.

As things turned out, there were no repercussions for the demonstration from the police or any disciplinary action by the school. Two police detectives visited the school a couple of times and spoke with the boy that stood up to speak at the District Commissioner's office, and that was it. This particular boy was not involved in organizing the demonstration, and it seemed that if he knew any of the organizers, he did not tell the police. The students also got the impression that the principal and the rest of the staff were impressed by and proud of the way the students had pulled off such a feat right under their noses and also by the students' intent not to disrupt their classes.

For a while at Tegwani, Kanda supplemented his pocket money by working for one of the teachers, Miss M, growing and tending to vegetables and flowers at her staff house. The arid soils of the area were not good for growing anything. For all his hard work and inventiveness, there was always not much to show for it. The teacher was, however, very nice and generous and paid him more for the effort than results. At the beginning, Kanda was embarrassed to be seen by the girls all dusty and dirty working in the garden. The teacher's house was by the road to the girls' dormitories. In time though, he made many friends among the girls who saw him working at the house. Some of them must have surmised where Kanda was coming from and where he was trying to get to. His employer later became Mrs. M when she married Kanda's favorite teacher, AB.

At the end of the third term in 1965, Kanda and a few other boys were offered a holiday job at the school for the whole of the December school holiday. This was a great and most opportune thing for Kanda for two reasons. The first was that he could not go home at the village for the holiday anyway. The last time he had gone home was the previous year's August holiday. A few days after his arrival at the village, there was a surprise police raid of the boys at his and other neighboring villages. The raid netted about twelve boys, including Kanda, and they were loaded onto police jeeps and taken to Bindura District police station. The purpose of the raid was to assess and deter nationalistic political activities among the youth in the area.

At the police station, the boys were placed in two separate cells. The police would take one boy at a time for interrogation. One tactic they used was to pretend to be friendly and to tell a boy that he was not one of the bad ones so that he could tell on the others. But most of the time, they were intimidating and threatening. For Kanda, who had just come home from boarding school, there wasn't much to offer the police. The food and cell conditions were terrible. A few days after the arrest, the parents of most of the boys, including Kanda's, followed to Bindura, bringing with them some food and warm clothing for the boys. The food was mostly bread, buns, Coke, and Fanta drinks. The boys were hungry and could clearly see the food the parents had brought. The parents were turned away and were not allowed to leave anything behind for the boys and were not even allowed to talk to them.

The boys were released after a week and were told to just leave and go back home by their own means. They ran most of the way home. About a week later, word came that a police convoy had been spotted headed toward the village again. This time, Kanda and the other village boys did not even try to hide around the homesteads as they had attempted to do the last time. They all dashed into the surrounding bush, never returning home that night for fear of being caught up in an ambush. Kanda got back home at sunrise, and his parents decided that he would not stay at the village any longer. The following morning, he was on the bus to Harare and on the train to Bulawayo to stay with his sister Getrude, who was now working together with Auntie D as a nurse at the Ingutsheni Mental Hospital. At that time and throughout Kanda's years at Tegwani, Getrude and Auntie D played a very significant role in meeting Kanda's school requirements.

The staff residence at the hospital itself was only for the female nurses, with the male and other married staff being housed at a separate residence about a kilometer away. Kanda would spend his daytime at the nurses' residence, where he would have his meals. In the evenings, he would go to one of the male staff houses, where sleeping accommodation had been arranged for him. Kanda also spent a lot of time away with his books at the park in the city. It was a lonely place for a young man to be, and his only contemporary at the residence, who became a close friend, was the beautiful daughter of one of the nurses who later left to train and work as a nurse in Britain.

The other reason why Kanda welcomed the holiday job was because his father had been struggling to keep up with the payment of his school fees. Kanda started each term without the full fees, which were then sent by mail as and when the money became available. So whatever money he would get from the holiday job, which was not disclosed to him beforehand, would be of great help. Staying at the school was also going to help him catch up with his studies.

The holiday job consisted mostly of painting the classrooms and other school buildings, with a general cleanup of the school premises. At the end of the holiday, Kanda was pleasantly surprised to be told that the holiday job had paid his school fees for the whole of his final year; the whole twenty-five pounds!

Kanda was aware that he had overstretched himself with his extracurricular activities, and he tried hard in the final year to focus on his academics. It was tough-going, and a few times, he stayed awake studying throughout the night. He struggled with mathematics, physics, and chemistry, all of which he considered very important for the future. The O Level Cambridge examination results came out early the following year, and Kanda had passed six subjects: English language, English literature, mathematics, biology, history, and Shona language and had failed physics, chemistry, and art.

During his final year at school, Kanda agonized over what he should do after high school, proceeding to form 5 and 6, and then university was completely out of the question due to the family's financial situation. There was a recently added limitation to his options, and it was imperative that he find a job and help support his siblings.

Early in 1966, Kanda's father ran away from home for fear of being arrested and placed in detention by the colonial government. He was an ardent nationalistic politician whose political activism, together with his colleagues Mavunga and Muzariri, was well-known in the Msana Native Reserve area. He was a very stubborn man when it came to politics. There was a time when the police, in a convoy of their jeeps, came for him at the village, and instead of feeling intimidated, he asserted his rights, demanding that he be allowed to go down to the river for a bath before they could take him. The police let him go to the river, and they followed behind and staked their positions near the river to guard him. He took his time bathing, walked slowly back to the house, and ate his breakfast before presenting himself to the police. Over a period, the police would visit him or his two partners to pick them up for short detentions or to just interrogate them as a form of intimidatory pressure on them. By 1966, however, the war of liberation, which was being directed from neighboring Zambia, was heating up, and the Rhodesian regime was now arresting and locking up nationalist politicians without trial for indefinite periods. Many prominent politicians in the country were caught up in this, and many more were fleeing to neighboring countries. Kanda's father's partner, Mavunga, who owned a shop at the Rutope Business Center, would later disappear and never to be accounted for. It was presumed that he was abducted and killed by the Rhodesian security forces, accused of assisting freedom fighters in the area with food and clothing. Muzariri was in and out of detention and died years later from Parkinson's disease.

For a while after Kanda's father fled the village, his family did not know where he was. It was presumed that he had fled the country as the other politicians were doing. It turned out, however, that he had gone into hiding in the remote Plumtree rural area, where his half-brother, Takawira, was employed as a caterpillar driver by the government Department of Roads Construction. Later, when the situation had quieted down, he moved to Bulawayo to his sister Maria until he could find his own place to rent. He remained in Bulawayo until his death one year after independence in 1981, before he could go back to the village, where his home and property had been destroyed during the war of liberation. After Kanda's father's departure from the village, his mother endured constant harassment from the police about her husband's whereabouts. There were also other issues at the village, which were beginning to make her life there unbearable, and she too left, taking with her the last born, Edson, then five years old, to live with her people at the Dombwe farm. Her departure left three children, Tennyson (fifteen), Florence (twelve), and Stanley (seven), on their own. Arrangements were made for Kanda's sister who comes after him, Mavis (seventeen at the time), to leave school so she could take care of the younger siblings at the village. Mavis had been at Msengezi Secondary School, a boarding school where she had been top of her Form 2 class. The departures of both Kanda's parents were thought to be temporary until things settled down, but this was never to be.

The same year that Kanda's parents left home, Kanda's sister Getrude, who had helped Kanda and the family financially, got married and was expecting her first child. She was leaving her job in Bulawayo to go and live with her husband in Harare. This was the family situation that confronted Kanda as he finished his high school in 1966. It was expected that he would immediately look for a job and take care of the family.

Kanda had wanted to be many things in life, which changed as he grew up. The one thing that he really wanted at this time, had he had the choice, was to join the ministry as a priest. Kanda grew up in a very religious family, and there had been recent experiences that reinforced his faith. Him leaving home without the money for fees and believing in prayer that God would provide was one of them. During his early years at Tegwani, he had suffered two medical conditions, which he believed were resolved by prayer. At one time, he suffered severe leg cramps. There was a well-known remedy among Kanda's people for the cramps, which was administered by herbalists, who the Europeans labelled witch doctors. A few razor cuts on the offending muscle and a rub-in of the witch doctor's ground herbs and one was good to go. When Kanda sought help from his father, the father would have none of that witch doctor treatment. He prayed and asked Kanda to do the same, and sure enough, the cramps disappeared. At another time, he experienced the problem of grinding teeth in his sleep. The grinding of the teeth was very noisy and a disturbance to the other boys in the dorm. Again, father and son prayed, and the problem eventually disappeared. Kanda's participation in the London Preachers Course and the chaplain's influence on him at Tegwani further reinforced his faith in Christianity.

Kanda's desire to be a priest was not a practical option. To begin with, he could not afford another period of training without money for himself and the family. Secondly, the priesthood did not pay well, so Kanda would not be joining the ministry. Kanda had also dreamed of becoming a medical doctor. He had applied and received a provisional admission offer from the University of Zambia. The University of Zambia accepted students after completion of O Level Cambridge examination only, whereas the University of Rhodesia required completion of form six or A Level examination. This option did not also appear to be viable for the same reason concerning money and also because Kanda was not doing well in his science subjects, which were a requirement to study medicine.

There was one other option that Kanda was considering. During the last term of his final year, there was a visit to the school by the principal of the School of Social Work, Father Rogers, a white Catholic Jesuit priest. He was seeking to recruit students to his School in Harare. Social work education was fairly new in Zimbabwe, which had relied on social workers trained in Britain, South Africa, and Zambia before the establishment of the School of Social Work in 1964. The first group of students that year started on a course of group work, which was a one-year practically-oriented course to help people to work with groups and the community. In 1966, a more comprehensive three-year course leading to the diploma in social work was launched. The school had a program of financial assistance through a government loan for students who could not afford the school fees and full board at the school's hostels at Westwood, the only multiracial suburb in Harare housing the students and some of the school's white staff.

Social work really appealed to Kanda, who had a yearning for a career of service born of his religious upbringing and his growing political consciousness. He and a few other students submitted their names to Father Rogers for consideration. He really wished he would be accepted by the School of Social Work, but the problem of his siblings at the village loomed large before him.

At the end of the final year, Kanda was selected to give the valedictory speech on behalf of the class of 1966. He gave an impassioned speech, which emphasized the students' responsibilities as they left school to enter the adult world. The whole issue of emancipating his people from colonial discrimination and oppression had become one of Kanda's preoccupations, and it dominated his speech, which was well-received by his classmates and staff.

Kanda at Tegwani with friends, Misheck to
the left and Robert in the middle

Kanda at Tegwani with buglers Edmund on
the right and Misheck in the middle

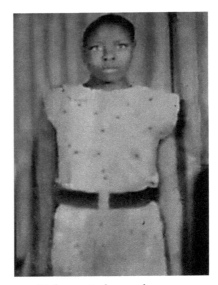

Rebecca in her early years

Getrude at Ingutsheni Hospital

Mavis behind the counter in her family shop

Tennyson and wife, Jennifer, at their church at the village

Florence with some of her grandchildren (2020)

Stanley at one of his graduations with Uncle Msande

Edson and wife, Patricia, at their wedding

Kanda's *chigadzanhaka* Benson and wife, Winnie (2020)

KANDA ENTERS THE ADULT WORLD

Wither to Kanda
All doors seemingly shut
Could it be as they say
When a door closes here
Somewhere, a window opens

As Kanda left Tegwani, he had to find some means of survival for himself and his siblings while he was in the process of looking for a job, whose prospects were very limited for African school leavers. At the village, he had an uncle named Sam, who was a few years younger than him and who bought and sold farm produce, mostly potatoes, at a market in Harare. The uncle bought the potatoes from the farms or from what was then known as the Eastlea Market at the eastern end of the city of Harare. He would sell them at the Market Square at the western end of the city, opposite the District Commissioner's office. The Market Square was where all the buses to and from the African townships operated from. It was a very busy place and a good one for the vending business, but the authorities did not allow vending there. For the vendors at the market, it was always a struggle of playing cat and mouse with the police, who constantly raided the vendors' goods. The potatoes that were bought from the farms were loaded onto the carriers of the rural buses coming into the city, and oftentimes, the police would be at the Market Square ready to impound them. This resulted in huge losses for the vendors. When this happened, the owners of the goods stayed away from their goods, not wanting to be associated with the contraband for fear of arrest.

Sam and some of the other vendors slept in an old disused building behind the District Commissioner's office to avoid the cost of rent and transport to and from the townships. The building that Sam and some of his fellow vendors occupied was built on stilts with a wide space between the ground and the building floor. The space was high enough for a person to crawl in and sit but not to stand. Sam and the other occupants called the place the cave. Only blankets and other bare necessities were kept at the cave as it was not safe for personal valuables. It was obviously not a clean place to live.

Kanda borrowed seven pounds from his grandmother, his father's mother, at the village and joined Sam at the Market Square and the cave. This was a desperate situation, and Kanda had to put aside any feelings of embarrassment at being seen in poor and dirty circumstances, vending at the Market Square, especially for a person who had just completed high school. The form 4 education was highly regarded then, and much was expected of the graduates.

Kanda's dilemma at the Market Square was that the best time for the vending business was in the morning when he would make his orders and stake out his vending spot at the market and also early evening when people were leaving work to board buses to the townships. But mornings were also the best time to look for jobs in the industries. So he decided to dedicate Monday as the day of the week when he would look for work all day. He would get to his sister Getrude's home in nearby Mbare (then Harare African Township) early in the morning, shower, eat breakfast, and set out to join the other job seekers in the nearby heavy industrial area in search of any available job. He would also use the time to send out job applications to government and other offices for clerical positions. Kanda would use the rest of the weekday mornings for vending. Around noon every day, he would leave his goods with Sam and walk to Mbare to shower, dress up, eat, and go job hunting in the industrial area until about 5:00 p.m. when he would return to Mbare and then back to the market for the evening vending. This was a gruesome and painful routine, especially in the absence of any positive or promising outcomes in the job search. There were no jobs to be found.

During his early days at the Market Square, Kanda became adept at avoiding people he knew, especially his former schoolmates. He would move away from his pile of goods and pretend to be a customer or to be passing by, or he would try and avoid any contact altogether. Over time, it became harder and harder to avoid people he knew, and eventually his vending spot at the market became the meeting point for his former classmates when they were in the city. It became common among them to tell each other that they would meet at Tim's place!

Kanda learnt a lot about vending from Sam, who had been in the business for several years. He learnt where to obtain the goods for sale, how to negotiate the buying prices, and how to set the selling prices according to changing market demands. Early on, he could not understand the auctioneer at the Eastlea market; it all sounded like "*halahalahala halahalahala ha*!" Sam would bid for him until he was able to follow the auction. Kanda also learnt not to bring all his goods directly to Market Square but to first take the goods to the cave and then bring them in small amounts to the market to avoid loss by police raids. At the Eastlea market, Sam and Kanda bought as much as they could carry. Kanda recalls many times when he would walk along Jameson Avenue (now Samora Machel), passing by the Reserve Bank of Rhodesia with sacks of potatoes on both shoulders on his way to the cave, unaware that he was engaged in an economic activity, which the Reserve Bank had a responsibility to account for. Also, little did Kanda know that he would one day be the occupant of an executive office on the nineteenth floor of a new ultra-modern Reserve Bank of Zimbabwe building as an advisor to the governor of the bank.

Kanda generated some moderate income from vending in spite of the ongoing harassment from the police. He kept constant contact with his siblings at the village and made sure they always had something to eat. He also bought some crop inputs and paid some of the villagers for help with ploughing and weeding the crop fields.

In early February 1967, Kanda received his O level results. He had passes in English language, English literature, mathematics, biology, history, and Shona language, and he failed physics, chemistry, and art. Later that month, he also got a letter from the School of Social Work offering him admission for the diploma in social work starting the following month, March 1967. Kanda really, really wanted to go to the School of Social Work, but he could not see how it could be possible when his situation demanded that he work and support his family.

One day, Kanda was discussing his dilemma with his school friend, Robert. Robert then suggested that Kanda could come and live with his family so that from his school loan, he could use the money that was meant for his full board at the school hostel to take care of his siblings at the village. Kanda could see the logic of it but was very uncomfortable about the idea of going to live and depend on a family of strangers for the whole time that he would be at the School of Social Work. He did not like the idea of being a burden on his friend's family. Robert's father was a priest, and his mother did not work, and there was Robert and his sister, Margaret, who were also not working at the time. When Kanda expressed his reservations, Robert insisted that he would talk it over with his parents. The next time they met, Robert told Kanda that his parents wanted to meet him and that they would be happy to have him stay with them while he went to school.

Robert's parents, Reverend and Mrs. Chihota, lived at the Methodist Epworth mission about fifteen kilometers out of Harare, where the reverend was the priest in charge at the mission. They lived in a modest three-bedroom house with running water and electricity. The reverend was a quiet person while the mother was quite outgoing. The family welcomed Kanda and informed him that they would be happy for him to live with them and that he would not be expected to pay anything during his stay. Robert would share his bedroom with him. Kanda liked the family, and he accepted the offer and thanked them for their generosity.

KANDA THE SOCIAL WORKER

An honorable career
To serve the people
Could it be a mirage

Kanda confirmed his acceptance of the offer of admission to the School of Social Work. He wound down his vending business at the end of February, and he left with a net profit of fourteen pounds. He paid back his loan of seven pounds to his grandmother. He used the balance on his siblings and himself as he prepared to return to school.

When school started, Kanda discussed his family circumstances with the principal of the School of Social Work while he was negotiating for an extra loan to buy a bicycle so that he could save on bus fare to and from the school and Epworth mission. After obtaining the full details of his situation, the principal got Kanda the extra loan. Later, unbeknown to Kanda, the principal approached Christian Care for assistance to pay Kanda's siblings' school fees. At that time, the Christian Care charitable organization was taking care of the children of African politicians who were arrested and detained by the colonial government. This came as a pleasant surprise because now all that Kanda needed to worry about was food and school uniforms for his young brothers and sisters. Father Rogers was no longer just Kanda's school principal but also his benevolent social worker, helping him solve some of his personal problems.

Kanda found cycling to and from Epworth quite challenging. The trip to school was a little lighter, but the return trip was steeper and harder. Kanda would also get to school tired, sweaty, and smelly.

Generally, among Kanda's contemporaries, cycling to and from the city was not the in thing (not cool) and was viewed as undignified and not endearing in the eyes of those of the fair sex. Kanda plodded on, and in time, he established a relationship with his acquaintances and the other passengers on the morning bus to the city. Kanda left Epworth way before the time of the bus he would have taken to go to school. Over time, the passengers on that bus got to know where the bus was likely to catch up with Kanda, and as they passed him, they would wave and call out to him through the windows to encourage him. What was once an embarrassment turned into fun, and each time this happened, it gave Kanda a bolt of energy in his cycling.

Kanda also used the bicycle for trips home at the village, a distance of about forty-five kilometers from Epworth, to check on his siblings. And again, the outgoing trip was easier than the return one, where the road was steeper on most parts and difficult for cycling. But the bicycle was a money saver.

Kanda really enjoyed his studies at the School of Social Work, especially the subjects of sociology and psychology. The overall environment at the school and relations with faculty were very pleasant. He felt that social work was indeed the right career choice for him.

By the end of the first year, Kanda had organized his finances in a way that allowed him to leave Epworth mission and join the other students at the school hostel at Westwood. He thanked his hosts at Epworth and left but maintained an ongoing relationship with his friend Robert and the family to this day. Kanda's life became more comfortable, giving him the chance to focus more on his studies. He kept his bicycle for some of his trips to the village.

For his three-month group work field assignment, Kanda was placed with a youth club run by the Bulawayo Municipality in the Makokoba African Township. The membership at this club was of young people around Kanda's age and was well-organized and well-run primarily by the club members themselves. The staff were there mostly to provide the resources and to ensure that everyone adhered to the club rules. Kanda didn't have much to teach or to input into the club's programs. Instead, he joined the club members in some of their activities, such as debating and practicing formal dancing.

He spent much of his time studying the group dynamics among the members as well as their programs and activities for future application in his studies and in his later work as a group worker.

For his casework field work assignment, Kanda was placed with the government Department of Social Welfare at its Highfield District Office in the Highfield African Township in Harare. This assignment was much more demanding and exciting than the group work assignment. Much of the work at this office was probation, working with juvenile criminal offenders and child welfare involving children in need of care. Though under the supervision of one of the established officers, the student was expected to go out in the field to investigate and assess cases and write reports for the juvenile magistrate courts. The actual presentation to the juvenile court of the reports prepared by the student would be done by the established officers, but the student was expected to attend court to hear the outcome and any follow-up orders by the court. There was a variety of possible outcomes for a juvenile convicted of a crime. The juvenile could receive a warning, a suspended sentence, a whipping or be placed under a probation officer's supervision for a period, usually three years. For the more serious cases, the juvenile could be sent to a probation hostel for a period. The hardcore offenders were placed in reformatories, which were more like halfway between the probation hostel and adult prison. Children in need of care were considered for foster care or adoption or were placed in institutions for children.

During Kanda's final year in 1969, the School of Social Work became the first associate college of the University of Rhodesia. On completion of his training, Kanda was awarded the diploma in social work by the university.

SOCIAL WORK IN COLONIAL RHODESIA

To serve Kanda's people, or
At the service of colonialism
What shall it be

Following the completion of his social work training, Kanda was offered the job of social welfare officer/probation officer by the government Department of Social Welfare at the Highfield District Office, where he had done his casework field assignment. The district officer had been impressed by the quality of Kanda's probation reports during his attachment, and Kanda was offered the job without the usual procedures of interviews. Kanda and another new female officer were the youngest in the whole Department of Social Welfare at the time. That village boy now had the title of officer to his name, which came with a whopping salary of sixty-eight pounds every month! There were sighs of relief everywhere in the family; the officer and first son of the family would now take care of the tribe!

Social work practice in colonial Rhodesia was very basic with a narrow view that fell far short of the philosophical foundations of the profession, whose primary aim is the promotion of the dignity and worth of people by helping them to resolve their problems and needs. It is a profession that, through the use of a variety of techniques, skills, theories, and methods, should assist people so that they can be able to assist themselves (Kurevakwesu, 2017). Instead, in colonial Rhodesia, social work practice was more for the benefit of the government rather than for the benefit of the people served. Social work was developed and practiced as a response to problems of crime, prostitution, and destitution in the urban areas. According to Kaseke (1991), the philosophy of colonial policy makers was that such ills, if left unattended, would undermine order and stability. Social work was, therefore, seen primarily as an instrument of social control and never seriously addressed itself to the root causes of social problems. The whole system was based on short-term fixes rather than long-term developmental approach to bring about desired social change. Mupedziswa (2015) gave the analogy of a leaking tap, whereby social work practice in colonial Rhodesia was like concentrating on mopping the leaking water rather than fixing the leaking tap.

The social welfare offices were segregated, with separate ones for whites and coloreds on one hand and for Africans on the other. It was always believed that the white and colored communities received better social services. The Highfield District Office was headed by a former military man who managed the office with the sternness of a military commander. The head of the district office was an indigenous African who had changed his name and was now living as a colored. The workload was heavy right from the beginning, and cases were assigned to Kanda and the other officers without consideration of the logistical problems faced by new officers, who did not yet have their own transport and relied on public transport. The cases were mostly from the various African townships that were spread out around the city. There were also cases involving domestic workers in the surrounding white suburbs. It took Kanda two years to obtain a driver's license so he could use the government car available at the office and before he could buy his own.

Most of Kanda's work was with the juvenile criminal offenders, with a little of child welfare caseload. There was not much public assistance work at the office. There was also not much help given to the destitute apart from giving them bus warrants to return to their rural homes, whether or not there were any support systems for them there. Kanda would meet with the offenders, their families, at times their neighbors or teachers if they were in school, and he would make his assessments and prepare reports for the juvenile courts. There was very little by way of resources or time for probation officers to offer their clients help beyond meeting the court requirements. There was not much time for follow-up with the juveniles to help them with their problems about such things as schooling, employment, or other social concerns. Unless offenders were placed under a supervision order, the officers' time with them at the courts would be the officers' last contact with them unless they reoffended. At times, it was frustrating and felt like a waste of everyone's time.

Kanda's work pressure improved considerably when he got his driver's license and could use the office car. He later bought his own car, a Hillman, the only one of its kind he has seen since. He could also now drive to the village at weekends or any time after work when necessary. The family situation at the village had since changed. His sister Mavis, whose dreams for a bright future had been shattered by being recalled from school in 1966 so she could take care of her younger siblings, got married in 1969, the same year Kanda was completing his training at the School of Social Work. A younger sister Florence, who was then fifteen years old, completed her standard six that year and was due to go to Usher secondary school for girls. With Mavis married and leaving, Kanda's father directed that Florence would no longer proceed to secondary school but would now remain at the village to take care of the boys. Kanda's younger brother, Tennyson (eighteen), now the oldest of the siblings at the village at the time, had not done well for his standard six and could not proceed to secondary school. His situation might have turned out differently with parental supervision. The other brother named Stanley (twelve) was still in primary school. The youngest, Edson (nine), was still away with his mother.

Florence did not last long at the village, and she got married in 1972. Tennyson then left the village to look for work and live with Kanda in Harare. Stanley was now in boarding school at Mazoe secondary school and came to Harare during school holidays. The damage that was occasioned by Kanda's family circumstances to the dreams and futures of the children, especially those of Mavis and Florence, is unimaginable. The two were very bright in school with potential for much greater things in life.

After four years with the government Department of Social Welfare, Kanda answered an advertisement by the municipality of

Kwekwe town for the position of welfare officer in charge of the welfare section of the African administration department. This type of work was the other side of social work; that is, group work as opposed to the casework he had been involved in. He went for the interview and was offered the job to start September 1974. This was a newly established position in the municipality and was later designated community services officer. The position was to be the highest post held by an African in the whole municipality. On appointment, Kanda was told that he was being taken on as a test case that would determine the future employment of other Africans. This notion turned out to be a gross under appreciation of the rapid political developments taking place in the country, because not long after, many other senior positions were being taken over by Africans who were replacing whites who were fleeing the impending majority rule in new Zimbabwe. Most of those whites were fleeing to apartheid South Africa, with others going to England and Australia.

Kwekwe was a medium-sized town just over two hundred kilometers from Harare and about halfway between Harare and Bulawayo. Its economy was dominated by large industries like ZISCO Steel, a powerhouse in the region, Sable Chemicals, Lancashire Steel, Rhomet, ZIMASCO, and the Globe and Phoenix Mine, where Kanda had come to live with his Uncle James in 1958. The municipality had two African townships, Mbizo and Amaveni, along with separate suburbs for whites and coloreds.

Mbizo and Amaveni African townships both had youth and women's clubs operating separately under the director of African administration, later redesignated as director of housing and community services. Kanda's task was to build a more professional and centralized community services function for both townships. He was responsible for the recruitment and training of the community services staff and for the formulation and promotion of various social, sporting, and community development initiatives for the youth, women, and other community organizations. Compared to his previous job, this was more challenging, requiring initiative, creative thinking, and new skills in management and community relations. In this new organization, he was the authority in his professional field, and he was also expected to be an example among the youths and the general township communities.

The new job came with an obvious benefit, a municipal rental house. This was a most welcome benefit as Kanda would now be able to bring his dependents to live with him in one place. In Harare, Kanda had lived in a pantry-size room in the Engineering Section of Highfield Township, which he had shared with his two younger brothers. Now he would have a full three-bedroom house with running water and electricity at Number 720 Mbizo African Township, just across the road from his new office. Kanda was able to immediately bring his brothers Tennyson, who was still looking for work, and Stanley, who was now completing his form 4 to live with him. The following year, he brought in his youngest brother, Edson, who had just completed standard six and was due to start form 1, and his nephew Benson, the son of Kanda's sister Rebecca. Rebecca, who had separated from Benson's father and had remarried, passed away that year, the same year that Kanda's paternal grandmother at the village had also died, leaving no one of Kanda's immediate family at the village. Later, Kanda was also able to bring his mother to live with them. The forced separation between Kanda's parents in 1966 eventually led to a permanent but unformalized separation, with his mother remaining with her people at the farm at Dombwe and his father living in Bulawayo with another woman as his wife.

Kanda set out to build the infrastructure of the department of community services. There was not much budgetary restriction on the number of staff, the equipment, and the resources he needed. At its peak, the department had a total staff of sixteen, including youth organizers, women's club mentors, bus drivers, and other support staff.

The previous approach to youth work here was not much different from the general philosophy of the government department of social welfare, which was more concerned with ensuring social stability and order with little long-term focus. Thus, the basic idea was to provide recreation that would get the youths off the streets and out of mischief. Kanda's challenge was to widen the scope beyond just recreation. The main youth activities had been soccer for the boys, net ball for the girls, movies at weekends, and cooking and sewing for the women. Kanda set out to expand these activities to include others with potential for future careers and income, such as arts and crafts and backyard income-generating projects. He also undertook counseling with the youths individually and in groups about their education, employment, and other challenges the youth faced as they grew up. On the women's side, he sought to expand their cooking and sewing sessions to include general hygiene, family health, childcare, and income-generating projects, with outside visits from various professionals coming to talk to them about these issues.

Overall, progress was slow, but with time, there was a definite shift from mere recreation to programs with a more long-term outlook.

In early 1978, the municipality recruited more Africans in senior positions, including township superintendents for the Mbizo and Amaveni Townships. Soon after, due to the rapid expansion of Mbizo Township, another position of assistant superintendent was created. Both the superintendent and the assistant positions were higher in terms of pay than that of Kanda. After failing to negotiate a higher salary for his position, Kanda applied and was offered the assistant superintendent position. The new position was more routine and less challenging than his previous one. The primary responsibilities were to assist with the allocation of the rented houses, rent collection, and evictions for nonpayment of rent.

THE NEW ZIMBABWE

Free at last, Free at last
Thank God almighty,
We are free at last.

—*Martin Luther King Jr.*

With the approach of political independence, there was an exodus of white people leaving government and other organizations throughout the country to emigrate. Kanda was keen to position himself for potential careers in the incoming majority-rule government. He needed the freedom to travel to Harare as and when it became necessary for job interviews. He particularly wanted a job in Harare as the seat of government and also because it would be closer to his home and the extended family. In 1979, he decided to leave his job with the Kwekwe Municipality and joined the Old Mutual at its Kwekwe branch as an insurance agent, a job that provided the freedom to travel. He was well-known in Kwekwe, and he started his new job with lots of potential prospects for his new insurance business, but he needed more experience and skills to close deals. Transient though the job was for Kanda, he thoroughly enjoyed it but also realized that sales work was really not the type of work for him. The effort to close a sale sometimes felt like arm-twisting a reluctant customer for their supposed benefit! Zimbabwe's independence came and went by in April 1980, and Kanda had not found the government job he desired.

The year that Rhodesia became Zimbabwe in 1980 was also the year that Kanda got married. He married late in life at thirty-five years old. Finding a suitable partner had not been easy for him. He was, of course, considered an eminently eligible bachelor, and over the years, there was no shortage of potential candidates for marriage. The first problem was that he had been more preoccupied with the upbringing of his siblings than focusing on his own personal needs. Related to that was the issue of finding a partner that would be willing and able to come in and assume the role of mother to an already large family of Kanda, his three brothers, a nephew, and mother. The time he met his wife, Rosemary, in 1977, however, all the philosophical restraining considerations were thrown to the wind! Their meeting was engineered by Kanda's dear friend, Charles, and it was love at first sight. Kanda and Rosemary could have married in 1978 but had to postpone the marriage due to an unfortunate family incident. The traditional marriage ceremony of payment of *lobola* was conducted the very month of Zimbabwe's independence in April 1980. The church ceremony and wedding celebrations were held on July 13, 1980. Theirs was the wedding of the year in Kwekwe, with a live band, plenty of food and drink, and the bride and groom and their attendants being driven in a posh convertible car belonging to Kanda's best man, Elias, his longtime friend from primary school.

Kanda was now a family man, and with no promising prospects for a job in Harare, he responded to an advertisement for the position of township superintendent for Mucheke, the only African township in the town of Fort Victoria (now Masvingo) in Masvingo Province. He was invited for interview and was offered the job starting August 1, 1980. Kanda became the first African superintendent for the Mucheke African Township, and the job was a real challenge. As he familiarized himself with the job situation, he realized that for many years leading up to Zimbabwe's independence, many people in the township had stopped paying their rents. There were tenants owing two to three years of rent, and the municipality had not been able to enforce the payment of rent! Also, compared to other African townships in other towns, Mucheke was among the least developed. It still had round huts under thatch for rent, and there was the amazing situation whereby a small round hut would be allocated to more than one person to share! One other problem that Kanda was going to deal with was that the many people who were now leaving the

African township to move to the former white suburbs wanted to retain their rented houses in Mucheke so that they could sublet them or reserve them for their relatives and friends at a time when there was a severe shortage of rental houses in the township. There was, at the time, pressure to provide accommodation for the many returning freedom fighters and other people who had been in exile outside the country.

Kanda's reception on his first day of work at the new office was a surprise. A dozen or so uniformed municipal police were lined up at the entrance to the office. The chief of the police saluted him and indicated that Kanda was expected to inspect the lined-up police, military-style inspection of the guard, with the chief leading the way. Kanda found all of this funny in a rather ridiculous way. He went along with this routine for a week and then decided to dispense with it as a relic of the colonial era. He, however, asked the chief to continue with the tradition on his behalf.

Kanda put the municipal police to work. Every morning, in addition to their normal daily duties, they would fan out throughout the township taking note of tenants who were leaving or had left for the former white suburbs. Kanda would then draw two lists, one of tenants with rent arrears and another of people leaving the township. He wrote down notes to people on the lists inviting them to come and see him at the office. The police delivered these notes to the respective houses. Kanda tried to see as many people as he could each day, and most days, he worked as late as 8:00 p.m. For those with rent arrears, he explained that the country was now in a new political environment with a people's government that expected the cooperation of all its citizens in order to move the country forward. For those leaving the township and wanting to retain their rented houses, he emphasized the duty of every citizen to ensure that the returning freedom fighters were properly received and accommodated. The response in both cases was very positive.

Not everyone was, however, pleased to be summoned to the superintendent's office. Kanda was new in Masvingo, and he did not know the people he was inviting to the office. Prior to independence no Africans were allowed to live in the white suburbs so that all the

African residents of Masvingo town lived in Mucheke Township, including some of the prominent politicians who were now in government and other institutions. Kanda was aware that some of the people he was inviting to come and see him might include some of these important persons. He was, however, confident that what he was doing was in good order, and he also had the backing of the ruling political party in the work that he was doing.

One day, one of the people he had invited to his office about the need to surrender his rented house was a well-known boisterous and volatile politician. Kanda's police must have deliberately not warned him about the man because they all wanted to see how he would react to the invitation. For them, it would be like watching a movie. The man came, not walking but marching with a pistol in hand. Kanda's police stood outside watching, amused. He stormed into the office. Kanda was taken by surprise, and he rose to greet him. The man, still standing, burst into a rant, wanting to know who Kanda thought he was to summon him to his office. Kanda did not know then who he was dealing with, and he kept on trying to explain the reason for the invitation. After a while, he calmed down and put the gun in his pocket but continued to stand and move about the office. He started laughing about his threatening behavior, telling Kanda that he was in fact doing a wonderful job. When Kanda eventually accompanied him out of the office talking nicely together, his staff was amazed.

There was another encounter with another prominent politician, but this one was a real gentleman. That man later became the speaker of the new Zimbabwe parliament. He responded to the invitation about giving up his rented house in the township. He came in, and Kanda explained the purpose of the invitation and what the office was trying to do to accommodate people coming back from the war and exile. The man was very appreciative of what the office was doing. Kanda would meet him again at a community function at a local Hellenic School, and he invited Kanda to check on him whenever he got to Harare.

During his encounter with people of Mucheke, Kanda could sense some general feelings of regionalism. People were always interested in knowing where he originally came from. In his previous job as assistant superintendent in Kwekwe, Kanda was used to seeing people who were invited to the office for nonpayment of rent being humble and apologetic before him in the hope for a reprieve or some other favorable consideration. At Mucheke, however, people who were invited to the office would come in, sit down in the visitors' chair facing Kanda, and invariably, they would first ask Kanda where he came from. "*Unobvepi mwanangu?*" Kanda could not help sensing some disappointment in their demeanor when he told them that he came from some other part of the country far away from Masvingo. There was also another related incident. There was a rumor that there was a young man, a relative of one of the local prominent politicians, who considered himself, presumably with some support in the community, as the one who should be in Kanda's position as superintendent of Mucheke Township. It was not clear if the young man had applied for the position when it was advertised and had failed to get the job. One day, a hefty young man came into Kanda's office, again with no forewarning from Kanda's staff. He sat down in the visitors' chair across Kanda's desk. He did not respond when Kanda greeted him. He just sat there staring at Kanda without saying a word. It was a very awkward and unnerving situation, and it went on for what seemed like a long time to Kanda. Finally, the young man stood up and left the office, again without even a word. Kanda learnt from his staff after he left that he was the young man who felt that Kanda was occupying his seat. Kanda was unfazed by this bizarre incident. He felt very secure in his job in which he had the full backing of the ruling party officials. He was also confident that the incoming first African Masvingo mayor, who was a fellow social worker, would have his back too.

Kanda was very fortunate to make the acquaintance of Joshua (not his real name), a well-known and influential figure in the Masvingo community. He was the first person to voluntarily surrender his rented house in Mucheke Township. He would be very useful in helping Kanda navigate some of the complex local political terrain. One weekend, Kanda can't recall if it was a Saturday or a Sunday, Kanda, Joshua, and their wives drove in Joshua's car to attend a political rally that was being held outside of Masvingo town in Gutu. The venue for the rally was a big, wide-open area with some hills on the sides. Present at the rally were the new Prime Minister Mugabe and many other senior government officials and politicians. Kanda and his group were seated in the VIP tent a few rows behind the prime minister. As superintendent of Mucheke, Kanda was recognized and accorded an elevated position in the local body politic. Being in the company of Joshua was also a factor in the VIP treatment he and his wife were accorded.

A short time into the rally, there was gunfire from the hills directed at the gathering. There was also return fire from the security forces who were providing security to the gathering. There was a scramble away from the clearing area. When there was a lull in the gunfire, people ran away into the surrounding bush and toward the parked cars. When the gunfire resumed, people would hit the ground and crawl away, a practice rural people had become accustomed to during the liberation war. It was a frightening and confusing situation, and Kanda's wife got briefly disorientated, running in the wrong direction where everyone was running away from, until Kanda grabbed her hand and redirected her. At the time, Kanda's wife was pregnant and in high-heeled shoes.

During the pandemonium, Mugabe was rushed to his armored car under heavy guard. As Kanda and the other people were all rushing to their cars, one senior politician kept on saying that a bullet had whizzed past his head and that he was lucky to have survived. He was saying it in a way that seemed to imply that he had been a target. Mugabe's convoy of cars and all the other cars left at high speed toward Masvingo town. Joshua's Jaquar joined the speeding convoy of cars. The plane that had brought Mugabe to Gutu was left behind at the local aerodrome. Once in Masvingo town, Kanda's wife was one of the women who served Mugabe refreshments. One naughty senior politician made a pass at Kanda's pregnant wife. Those familiar with the politicians in Masvingo would readily know who this naughty man was!

The incident that took place in Gutu that day remains a mystery and was never reported in the newspapers, on radio and television, or in any other media to this day. For most of the country, it's like it never happened. It is also unknown who was responsible for the attack and why and whether or not there were any injuries or fatalities.

From the time that he took his job in Masvingo, Kanda had not stopped his search for a job in Harare. He had now widened his search beyond just government employment. In December 1980, he responded to an advertisement for a personnel officer position at the Harare branch of the Zimbabwe Sugar Refineries (ZSR). He was invited for interview and was offered the job starting February 1, 1981.

Sometime after Kanda left Masvingo, he had a chat with one of his uncles about his experiences in Kwekwe and Masvingo. It later turned out that his uncle had somehow formed the impression that Kanda had been forced out of his job at Mucheke Township due to tribalism. This was in fact not correct because during the time that he was in Masvingo, Kanda had been busy looking for any available opportunity to move to Harare. Anyway, in one of the uncle's conversations with Mugabe, a longtime friend of his from when they were both teachers, the uncle must have passed on his impression about Kanda's departure from Masvingo. Mugabe then asked his friend to find out if there was a government job that Kanda might be interested in and was qualified for. When his uncle came back to him, Kanda explained the correct position about his departure from Masvingo but still welcomed the opportunity to be considered, at the highest level in the country, for a career in the new government. So he prepared his application, in long hand then, seeking an appointment to any position for which his educational qualifications and work experience were appropriate in the diplomatic services abroad. *Why not go for the real thing, given a chance?* he thought. Kanda handed his application to his uncle, who confirmed it had been passed on to the prime minister. Kanda alerted his wife of the possibility of an overseas posting. Weeks went by, and there was no news about the application. Weeks turned into months and still nothing. People kept telling Kanda to be patient, assuring him that Mugabe was known not to forget promises he made. Nothing ever came out of it.

Kanda's job at the Zimbabwe Sugar Refineries was another pioneering work. The company had two branches, one in Harare and the other in Bulawayo. The Bulawayo branch had a branch personnel office and a personnel officer. The Harare branch had a labor office, which was primarily tasked with the recruitment of temporary laborers from outside the company gates as needed, with most of the other personnel work being carried out by the personnel manager at head office in Harare. Kanda was the first personnel officer for the Harare branch and was tasked with developing the branch personnel office into a fully-fledged professional personnel function. He was responsible for the recruitment and training of the non-managerial employees at the branch, the updating and maintenance of personnel records, reviewing and updating of discipline and grievance handling procedures, development of performance appraisal and incentive systems, assistance in the review of wages, and working with the workers' committee on matters of discipline, wage increases, and other worker concerns.

Kanda's first trip to the Bulawayo branch was in September 1981 by plane, his first time to fly. The visit was a one-day trip, early in the morning to Bulawayo and back in the evening. When he got onto the plane, he was busy looking for a vacant place to sit when he was informed that the seat allocated to him would show on his boarding ticket. The trip was simply to familiarize Kanda with the branch operations, especially the personnel office. At the lunch break, his counterpart at the branch offered to drive Kanda to Makokoba Township to see his father. Kanda had a brief time with his father, whom he had not seen for quite some time and who looked frail. He informed his father that he was going to start rebuilding the family homestead at the village so that he could come back home, and his father cautioned him to wait until after the rains in the New Year. That was to be the last time Kanda saw his father. Two weeks after the visit, he received a message that he had died of a stroke on the way to the hospital in an ambulance. Kanda and the family buried him at the village.

Kanda's mother was still living at the house in Mbizo Township, which Kanda had since bought through a newly introduced home ownership scheme. Tennyson was now working for the Kwekwe Municipality and was now married with his own rented accommodation. His brother Stanley had just completed his university engineering degree and was now working but still living with Kanda and his wife. Edson had completed his Form 4 and was looking for work and still living with Kanda. The nephew, Benson, did not qualify to proceed to secondary school after completing his Standard Six and was now looking for work and living with an uncle in Mbare Township.

Kanda enjoyed his work at the Sugar Refineries and was well-respected by both his seniors and the rest of the employees. Then, one day toward the end of his first year, a friend of his, Brian, also a personnel officer at the Air Zimbabwe head office in Harare, mentioned that there was going to be an opening for a personnel officer at the airline and that the job would be advertised in the newspapers soon. Kanda had always wanted to travel the world and a job at the airline, and its travel benefits was very appealing. As he watched out for the newspaper advertisement, Kanda saw one that said a large commercial organization was looking for a personnel officer. The advertisement was through a recruitment agency run by a married couple, David and Angela. Kanda called the agency and spoke with Angela. When he asked to know the organization that was advertising the job, he was told that that information would only be availed to short-listed applicants. Kanda then asked Angela if she would be able to tell him yes or no if he told her who he thought the organization was, and she said she would be happy to do so. When Kanda mentioned Air Zimbabwe, Angela said it was definitely not the organization. Kanda thanked her and was about to hang up when Angela suggested that he still consider the job that they were advertising. He told her that he was not unhappy where he was but that he had been interested in the particular job at the airline because of its travel benefits. Angela kept the conversation going, asking Kanda his qualifications and work experience. She then invited him to come in for a chat, saying he had nothing to lose by the visit. Kanda agreed and went to see her with his resume and other supporting documents. During the interview, she disclosed that the job was at the Reserve Bank of Zimbabwe and that it came with many benefits, including housing and personal loans, noncontributory pension scheme, non-contributory medical aid scheme, and financial assistance to further one's education. At the time of this interview, Kanda had been having trouble finding suitable and affordable accommodation and had moved from one rental place to another four times since he moved to Harare a year ago. The benefits that came with the Reserve Bank job were very attractive, especially the loan scheme to buy a house. Kanda was sold to the job, and he let Angela know.

Angela arranged an interview for Kanda and the representatives of the Reserve Bank at her offices. On the appointed day, two white gentlemen in black suits and with black briefcases entered the offices. *It was real serious business here*, Kanda thought to himself. The gentlemen introduced themselves to Kanda as the bank secretary and the personnel manager. The interview went well, and Kanda was told that he would be informed of the decision soon. Kanda could not wait for this decision!

Kanda was offered the job to start May 2, 1982. He later learned that the bank secretary and the personnel manager had already made up their mind on another candidate but were so impressed by Kanda during his interview that they decided to go back and seek authority from the board for another personnel officer position. The other candidate was a white lady who had been a personal assistant to a company personnel manager and was studying for the diploma in personnel management through the Institute of Personnel Management of Zimbabwe. Although both positions had the same title of personnel officer, Kanda was appointed as a junior to the white lady. It was here at the Reserve Bank of Zimbabwe that Kanda would settle down and stay for the next twenty years.

The Reserve Bank was a different type of work environment for Kanda. Again, he was the first African personnel officer in the organization, and for the first time, his responsibilities now involved people of all races. The personnel department was new, with the personnel manager having been recently recruited from government, where he had been a principal administration officer. Although Kanda did not have any direct qualifications in personnel management, he was probably the most qualified in this new personnel department in terms of working with people on the basis of his social work training and experience and his one year of personnel work practice.

Prior to the establishment of the personnel department, all personnel-related matters were handled by the bank secretary and his staff. Up to 1982, the bank was a small organization of about three hundred employees. With the coming of independence, the bank was expanding. After a few years, the number of employees doubled, and years later at its peak, the number of employees more than tripled. The immediate task of the personnel department was the review and development of professional personnel policies and procedures in the areas of recruitment, training, promotions and transfers, discipline and grievance handling, salary administration, performance appraisal, communications, and record keeping and maintenance. On a day-to-day basis, most of Kanda's work was recruitment of new employees, counselling, assisting staff with loan applications, participating in performance appraisal follow-ups, and participating in job evaluation exercises. He was also involved in discipline and grievance matters and working with the workers' committee.

Kanda qualified for the housing loan benefit at the completion of his first year at the bank. After some extensive house search, he and Rosemary settled for a property in the exclusive northeastern suburb of The Grange in the Chisipite area. It was a three-bedroom house on one and a quarter acre plot, with a large swimming pool and a borehole with an underground sprinkler system. There was an outer building comprising a double lockup garage, two storerooms, a workshop, and domestic workers' quarters. The house was at the end of an avenue with open space at the back and on one side. At the time, Kanda and Rosemary had one child, Kuda, born November 1982. The other two would follow in 1985, Tatenda, and Mutsa in October 1986. Kanda's other child before marriage, Cynthia, who lived with her mother until she completed primary school education, would later come and join the family in 1992 and go to high school. Kanda also brought his mother from Kwekwe to live with them for a while before she returned to the village, where Kanda and his brothers were rebuilding the family homestead. The Grange was a beautiful place to live and raise a family.

In September 1983, the personnel manager resigned from the bank to emigrate to Australia. At about the same time, Kanda transferred out of the personnel department. Some people thought that his transfer was somehow connected with his boss's departure. That the two happened at the same time was just a coincidence. Kanda did not seek the transfer. Among the people Kanda recruited were candidates for the position of assessor in the exchange control department, mostly university graduates. Recruits who were successful at interview were then put through a screening test that was conducted by an outside agency. One day, Kanda decided to take the test so he could have a feel of what he was putting his recruits through. Normally, all the test results were sent back to him or the other personnel officer. This time, the testing agency sent all the test results to him except his. It turned out the agency had withheld Kanda's results and sent them directly to the head of the exchange control department, who, in turn, was impressed by the results and had gone to the bank secretary to ask that Kanda be transferred to his department. Kanda's superiors must have assumed that he took the test because he was interested in the job, and the decision to transfer him was made without any consultation with him. Once that decision was made, however, Kanda actually looked forward to the opportunity to be exposed to one of the main operations of the bank. He had also not been happy about being junior to the other personnel officer in the personnel department.

The exchange control department was responsible for the allocation of the country's scarce foreign currency to businesses and the general population for various purposes, such as remittance of dividends, pensions, school fees, medical treatment, business and personal travel, people emigrating, and so on. The exchange control assessors, as the name suggests, processed the applications that came to the Reserve Bank through the commercial banks and approved or recommended the allocation of the foreign exchange. Most of the cases were routine, with the exception of corporate cases which were complicated and required some accounting knowledge to understand the underlying financial transactions in the business applications. Kanda enjoyed his work and remained in the exchange department until 1985 when he was called back to the personnel department. Before he left the exchange control department, he wrote a lengthy paper with recommendations on some of the exchange control policies. He felt very strongly about some of the items on which the scarce foreign exchange was being expended. One particular area that Kanda felt should be reviewed was the allocation of foreign exchange for children's university fees abroad in cases where the studies being pursued were readily available in the country. Many of the assessors were in agreement with Kanda's views, but his paper was considered too controversial to forward to senior management, most of whom were personally benefiting from this policy. The paper was kept in the circulation file on the floor and was never passed on to senior management.

In 1985, the bank appointed another personnel manager, an African a few years younger than Kanda but with many years of personnel management experience. When the new personnel manager got to know about Kanda, he asked that he be brought back to the personnel department. Kanda was transferred back to the personnel department. He was transferred on promotion to the position of senior personnel and training officer. The lady personnel officer had been transferred out of the department.

The personnel manager was a charming and unassuming man who became more of a mentor than a boss to Kanda. He introduced Kanda to some of the new ideas and developments in the field of personnel management and allowed him a lot of latitude for him to show what he was capable of. With the expansion of the bank, more personnel were appointed to the department. The department was later redesignated to human resources department, and in 1987, Kanda was promoted to the position of manager of human resources, with several human resources officers and support staff below him.

Every year, the bank held a managers' conference at some the country's most attractive holiday resorts, such as Nyanga in the eastern highlands, Victoria Falls, and Kariba. Nyanga has beautiful scenery and weather and has been nicknamed Little England. Victoria Falls is one of the seven wonders of the world, and Lake Kariba is the world's largest man-made lake. The managers' conferences were attended by all levels of management. The conferences were characterized by departmental reports covering reviews of past performances, some forecast of future needs, and problems and proposals for the future. In 1987, the conference was held at Nyanga, and Kanda was in attendance for the first time. The managers were accompanied by their spouses, and Rosemary was also there at the conference. A special nonbusiness program was always prepared for the spouses while the managers attended to the business of the bank.

Kanda's boss had allowed Kanda to prepare and make the presentation on behalf of the personnel department at the conference. His presentation was a diagrammatic representation of staff moves in the bank based on actual data for the previous year. The bank had fifteen job grades from the cleaner at the bottom to the top. The diagram showed all the people that joined the bank from outside at each grade level, the number of all the people that left the bank at each grade level, all the promotions and demotions from one grade to the other, and all the internal transfers at the same grade levels. Kanda then pointed out that if those data were interposed with the ages of the people involved and their education, experience, and skills, the result would be a clear picture of the well-being of the organization as a living organism. The information would also highlight the impact of the human resources decisions in areas such as recruitment, training, promotions, transfers, pay and retention schemes, retirement, etc. The presentation generated a lot of interest among the managers, and at one point, the governor of the bank had to take a phone call, and he asked Kanda to pause until he finished his call. At the end of the presentation, the governor made the remark that maybe the bank should send Kanda for a human resource planning course. Kanda would take him up on his word.

Back at the bank, Kanda discussed the governor's remark with his boss, who was also in favor of him going for the human resource planning training. The boss suggested that Kanda apply to the Polytechnic of Central London in England, where he had once been offered a place that he was not able to take up. The Polytechnic of Central London, later renamed the University of Westminster, offered a one-year masters' degree in manpower studies, which was basically human resource planning at both the macro (country) level and micro (organization) level. Kanda applied, and he was offered admission to start September 1988. He submitted his application for study leave and financial sponsorship to attend the University of Westminster in 1988. He was granted both fully paid study leave and financial sponsorship for the study. Kanda's wife and children would also be sponsored to visit him in London for two weeks. Kanda became the first employee of the Reserve Bank of Zimbabwe to be fully sponsored by the bank for full-time study anywhere at home or abroad.

Kanda's trip to London was his second outside the country. The previous year, he had traveled to Tanzania to attend a five-week management training program conducted by the Eastern and Southern African Management Institute (ESAMI) at Arusha Town. Fearful of the security of its staff, the bank had arranged with the Zimbabwe Embassy in Dar-es-Salaam to meet Kanda at the airport and to accommodate him overnight before his connecting flight to Arusha up north. All that precaution turned out to have been unnecessary, but Kanda did not know then. At Arusha, as he was looking for a taxi to take him to ESAMI, a man took Kanda's luggage and led him to his taxi, an old matatu with plastic coverings on some of the windows. ESAMI was some way out of town, and as they drove out of town, the driver must have noticed Kanda's discomfort and misapprehension in his demeanor, and he pointed in the direction of ESAMI, and Kanda was relieved to see the familiar image of ESAMI on the hill as it appeared on the institute's brochure. The one thing Kanda cannot forget about ESAMI was the smell of the local coffee, and one could smell its rich aroma on approaching the premises. Kanda and the other participants spent a lot of their free time in Arusha town, which had some nice night spots, including Saba Saba (77 in Swahili) and Arusha by Night. The weather was beautiful. Kanda fell in love with Arusha, and he left the country with the impression that the people of Tanzania were among the nicest in the world.

Kanda would return to Tanzania years later and visit some of its renowned game parks at Serengeti National Park, Manyara National Park, and the Ngorongoro Crater. The Ngorongoro Crater is a great wonder of nature's creation, a whole world of an assortment of animal life, both prey and predator, in a colossal depression in the earth.

Kanda's trip to London had some moments of drama. The Air Zimbabwe flight to London normally left in the evening, arriving in London early morning the following day. Kanda boarded his flight on Friday, September 23, 1988. He had a window seat, and next to him was an Asian man who owned a chemist shop at corner Kingsway and Jameson Avenue. After a short while, the flight signs indicated people could unbuckle their seat belts and that passengers could smoke. Kanda and the man next to him lit their cigarettes and started chatting. The two must have missed an announcement because a cabin attendant came rushing to them asking what they were doing still smoking. She asked them to look outside. There was what appeared like a stream of fire stretching the whole length of the plane to the back. Kanda had always been made to understand that a fire near an airplane was dangerous, and here was a red-hot gush of fire spreading along the plane while it is in the air! It turned out that what Kanda saw outside was fuel being released from the plane's tanks. The flight crew had seen a flash signal indicating that the luggage compartment door was not securely closed. The plane had to turn back to Harare airport to have the problem fixed before proceeding on the journey, and it was necessary to lose some of the fuel so the plane would have the proper weight for landing. So the plane went round and round for quite a while before landing. Kanda was still on the Zimbabwe soil when his family thought he was way away on his way to London. The plane took off again after about two hours.

Kanda had heard about the extreme cold weather conditions and snow in England. He anticipated that it might be very cold when he arrived in London. He had bought a three-quarter winter coat for the trip. Kanda traveled with all his money for school fees, full board at the college's student hostel, and for his other living expenses for the year. The money was in the form of travelers checks to be cashed as needed. He had bought a small black purse with a looped band for holding it, and he carried money, ID card, and passport in the purse, which he put in the inside pocket of his winter coat. When he got to

London, he would need to keep the winter coat on for the security of his valuables until he was in a safe place. He had five pounds in cash for the trip and one-day coupons for train and bus travel in London. He checked in his suitcase at the airport and kept his briefcase with him, and he was ready for London.

Before his flight at the Harare airport, Kanda was introduced to a young man named John (not his real name), who was returning to London after a holiday in Zimbabwe. John was to help Kanda find his way when they got to London. From his previous air travels, Kanda was used to seeing one luggage carousel operating at the airports. So after disembarking at Gatwick Airport, he stopped at the first luggage carousel he saw and waited for his luggage. John had to come and get him, explaining that they should check for their flight number on the many display screens for the right carousel for their luggage. They then took the Gatwick Express to Victoria Station. When they went to board the underground train, John noticed that what Kanda had was a coupon and not an actual ticket to board the train. John directed Kanda to go back and exchange the coupon for the ticket at the Victoria Station ticket office. John apologized that he was in a hurry and could not accompany him or wait for him. Kanda was now on his own in London. He spent some time looking for the ticket office. He learned his first lesson about asking for directions in London. Invariably, Londoners will tell you it's 'round the corner, and they are done with you. He learned not to assume people in London know their surroundings. He finally located the ticket office, got his ticket, and went back down to the tube train.

Kanda had some misconceptions about the tube train. He had heard stories that its doors opened and closed very quickly so that if you were not careful, you could get squashed between the doors as they closed or get separated from your luggage as you boarded the train! Thus, when he got to the train platform, he was kind of pushing and shoving to position himself well for when the train came. He must have been a spectacle to the people around him. It was a hot day, and he had his winter coat on, fully buttoned, and he was in a hurry to get in front of everybody. They must have wondered what this dude from the Motherland was up to! And sure enough, when the train arrived, he was among the first to jump in. The train was full with standing room only. He had his suitcase, his briefcase, and his tube map in hand. He showed the map to someone next to him and asked if he would let him know when he got to his destination. Information has meaning only within the right frame of reference and in the context of the known. The anxiety that results from the uncertainty of a strange and unfamiliar environment can impair mental orientation and the processing of information that may be available. Kanda had the tube map in his hand. There was also a tube map on the sides of the train above the windows, and each station was announced as the train approached it, yet Kanda was still anxious that he might miss his destination and get lost and stranded in London. Anyway, when he finally saw on the map that his station, the Great Portland Street, was next, he moved forward, ready to disembark. He got off the train and climbed up to ground level outside. The directions to the college hostel were quite clear, right onto Bolsover Street and one hundred yards down the street. Kanda was used to street signs on posts slightly above eye level. It took him some time to locate the street name, which was way up on the wall of a tall building. Kanda had always known that he was somehow short-sighted, and it was here that he realized he needed eyeglasses to see properly. He followed Bolsover Street and got to the address of the student hostel. He had finally arrived at his destination in London.

There were two employees at the hostel responsible for admitting students to the hostel. They informed Kanda that he was required to pay a deposit of five pounds and five shillings for admission to the hostel. He had only five pounds in cash and asked if he could be let in and he would pay the balance when he has had time to cash his travelers' checks. The employees insisted that the full amount had to be paid before he could be allowed in. By the time he got to the hostel, it was past noon, and the banks had already closed. He was directed to a nearby hotel where he could cash his travelers' checks. The hotel staff said they only cashed travelers' checks for people booked at the hotel. They suggested that he try a place whose name to Kanda sounded like *burodishe* down along a street that sounded like *marybo*. Following the directions that he had been given, Kanda realized that what sounded like *marybo* was actually Marylebone Street, and *burodishe* was bureau de change! He went down Marylebone Street and saw the bureau de change, with the Madame Tussauds's dome appearing further down the road to the right. There was a man at the window of the bureau de change chatting with the cashier inside. The man stepped aside when Kanda arrived but did not leave, making Kanda uncomfortable that he should get some large amount of cash with this stranger looking on. He was not sure too how much he needed for his immediate needs and when he would next be able to get some more cash. He then decided to cash one thousand pounds worth of the travelers' checks. He put the money in his purse and in the inside pocket of his coat. It was still hot, and Kanda was still fully buttoned up to protect his valuables.

About halfway on his way back on Marylebone Street, one car driver suddenly stopped in the middle of traffic, literally, and started beckoning to Kanda to come over to him. Kanda could not imagine anyone who might recognize him here and a white man for that matter. When he looked around, there was nobody else but him alone. He asked "Me?" using sign language, and the man indicated in the affirmative. Kanda signaled for him to come to the edge of the road so they could talk. The first thing the man did was to ask "Are you from Nigeria?" Kanda told him he was from Africa, but not from Nigeria. The man who introduced himself as Antonio told Kanda that he helped foreign students with affordable winter jackets. He asked Kanda to jump into his car so he could take him where he, Kanda, was going and show him the jackets. Kanda was wary of getting into the car of a stranger who might hijack and rob him and dump him some place. He asked Antonio to meet him at the hostel, and he was already there when Kanda arrived. He showed Kanda the jackets, which were made of synthetic leather with thick cushioning inside. Kanda was interested in the jackets but was not sure about the pricing. The hostel staff assured him that the prices were reasonable, and he bought one for about five pounds. Kanda would later meet Antonio again several times around London at places where there were students. At one such occasion, Antonio agreed to exchange, at no extra charge, the jacket that he had sold Kanda with another one that Kanda thought was better.

Kanda paid his deposit, and the hostel staff showed him his room, the size of his pantry back home, in the basement. The hostel was a self-catering facility, and Kanda needed to set himself up with some kitchen utensils and food stuff. He asked the hostel staff for directions to the nearest shopping center. He followed the directions he was given and found himself at Oxford Street, the premier shopping center of the world, with hundreds of pounds in his pocket! When he asked for directions to a shopping center, he did not explain what he wanted to buy, and so the hostel staff directed him to the Oxford Street shopping district. What he had in mind was a place like the Machipisa shopping center in Highfield Township or the Chisipite shopping center where one could buy kitchen utensil and groceries. On the way, Kanda had noticed small shops labeled food and wine, and on his way back to the hostel, he got into one of these shops only to find what he was looking for. He bought a pot, a pan, and other smaller utensils and some food items and drinks. When he asked for mazoe orange crush, the shop attendant had no idea what that was. Mazoe orange crush was a product of the Mazoe Citrus Estates in Zimbabwe and was popular in Zimbabwe and the surrounding region, and Kanda had somehow assumed that it would be available everywhere, like Coca Cola and Fanta!

As a small child, Kanda was very religious, and the whole idea of going to heaven was a big deal for him. But if he had been asked then where he would prefer to go, London or Heaven, his answer would have been unequivocal: heaven via London! He could not conceive of a life without ever been to London. From the stories that he grew up hearing, London was second only to heaven in its glory. Thus, his first impression of London was very disappointing and nowhere near what he had imagined as a child. As they landed at Gatwick Airport, Kanda looked out the window, and the airport below looked like a junkyard, with what appeared to be odd pieces of equipment strewn all over the place. On the Gatwick Express to Victoria Station, his first impression of the place was an array of chimneys, rows upon rows of chimneys in all directions as far as the eye could see. He thought they were passing through an industrial area before he realized that the chimneys were on the rooftops of residential houses. When they got to London, there was dog poop everywhere on the streets. And this was supposed to be central London, the heart of the mighty British Empire! One had to do a kind of hop step-and-jump routine to avoid stepping on the dog poop. Kanda had never seen any dog poop on the streets of Harare. Even at the village the dogs, like the humans, hid their poop in the bush. The buildings were old and dull. The rows of red brick buildings where he was staying reminded Kanda of the huge tobacco barns you saw on white commercial farms in colonial Rhodesia. There was always some patchwork going on everywhere on the roads. The weather was like it was in a bad mood every day. On the buses and trains, the English did not talk or look at each other and pretended like you were not there. If as a child, Kanda had known this, his answer to that question of preference would have also been unequivocal: straight to heaven!

The next weekend after his arrival, Kanda's friend Bonny came to see him and to take him on a tour of London in his car. Bonny was a year behind Kanda at the Tegwani Institute and later at the School of Social Work. He grew up in Highfield Township, where his father was a businessman. He and Kanda used to go out in Kanda's car to drink and meet with friends. One day after an evening out, they were just chatting and came up with the idea that since Bonny did not have family responsibilities to worry about at the time, why not ask Father Rogers of the School of Social Work to recommend him for a job in the United Kingdom and use that to test the acceptability of the School of Social Work diploma abroad? Father Rogers was agreeable, and he connected Bonny to the Social Services Department of the city of Reading in England. He came to England in 1973 and was working for the city of Reading as a social worker and furthering his education. At the time of Kanda's arrival in London, he was studying for his doctorate in criminology.

The first place they visited was Buckingham Palace. Kanda could not help wondering whether the gold he saw on the Buckingham Palace gates might have come from the Globe and Phoenix Mine in Kwekwe or some other gold mine in Zimbabwe. This was quite possible because he had seen at one of the tube stations an inscription RISCO Steel on the steel rails of the subway railway line. RISCO was Rhodesia Iron and Steel Company (now ZISCO) in Kwekwe, Zimbabwe. The railway system in London, or at least part of it, was made from steel obtained (possibly looted) from Rhodesia when it was a colony of the British.

Bonny showed Kanda many other places of interest, including the Houses of Parliament, Big Ben, and the London Bridge. Kanda was impressed by how well Bonny navigated the narrow streets of London using a printed map. There was no GPS yet at the time. They also visited Soho, where Kanda had a culture shock from the vast array of explicit pornographic material on full display in public. In the weeks that followed, Kanda continued to explore London, visiting places like the Harrods, Madame Tussauds, and the Africa Center at Covent Garden, the closest place to Africa in London.

On the first day of school, Kanda was the second person to arrive in class. Before him was a beautiful young lady who introduced herself as Noreen. After exchanging greetings, Noreen asked Kanda where he came from. When he told her that he was from Zimbabwe, she was surprised and told him they both came from the same country. She said in Kanda's home language, *"Inga uri mwana wekumusha,"* which means "You are my homeboy." Noreen was already living and working in London. She told Kanda that another Zimbabwean had attended the same class the previous year. As the other students came in, it turned out that the whole class was made up of international students with the exception of one British. The one-year manpower studies program was highly intensive, covering the areas of corporate manpower decisions, manpower studies, organizational analysis, manpower planning, intervention skills, manpower planning examination, and manpower planning thesis. The study program was heavy on statistics and statistical analysis. Because of Kanda's problem generally with mathematics, he had anticipated some problems in this area but was happy to find out that applied statistics as opposed to pure mathematics was much easier and quite enjoyable.

The manpower examination and the manpower planning thesis had to be completed within the one-year program, and this put pressure on Kanda as any request for extension of time would not be looked at with favor back at the bank. He thus started preparing for the thesis early in the year. His thesis, which was to be titled "A Looming Crisis of Expectation: The Analysis of an Anticipated Crisis of Promotion Expectations in the Reserve Bank of Zimbabwe," was based on actual Reserve Bank employee data for the years 1987 and 1988. He had brought some of the data with him, and some more were being sent from the bank as needed.

Kanda's thesis was proposing that there was a looming crisis of promotion expectations in the bank and that the prevailing rapid promotions would slow down in the near future so that promotion expectations would far exceed the opportunities available to accommodate them. The situation being studied arose from two main factors, both attributable to Zimbabwe's attainment of political independence, which are the rapid growth of the bank and the exodus of white senior staff. The two factors and the indigenization of staff in the bank in line with the prevailing practice at the national level led to the speedy promotion of young Africans into senior positions that, under normal conditions, would have taken them many years of training and experience to reach. It was thus anticipated that the problem of unfulfilled promotion expectations would take three interrelated forms. The first would concern the young people already occupying senior positions but with little opportunity for further advancement. Following from this would be the problem of staff in lower grades, whose chances for upward movement would be blocked by young people in senior positions above. The third problem would stem from the high level of expectations generated by the current speed of promotions, which would not be possible to maintain. Kanda's task was to analyze the data and to produce quantifiable statistical results to prove the proposition.

In July 1989, amid his busy schedule with class work, homework assignments, and the thesis, Kanda had to attend to another very important thing to him: to receive and entertain his wife and children who had come to visit him for two weeks. It had been the longest time that he and his family had been separated, and it was a joyful reunion. His hostel room was too small to accommodate his family, so he rented a small apartment nearby. Kanda took his family sightseeing and shopping around London. There were two things that put a dent on the holiday mood. The first was the weather; July that year experienced record heat in London. The second was that the youngest of the children, Mutsa, fell ill. The heat was probably a factor in her condition. Kanda and Rosemary spent considerable time with her at the Brompton Children's Hospital, and there were also some doctor's follow-ups by phone. Due to Kanda's student status, there was no charge for the hospital visits and the doctor's follow-up time. Among the items that Kanda bought for the children were bicycles. As soon as he saw the bicycles, the son, Tatenda, who was four then, was no longer interested in staying in London and wanted to return to Zimbabwe so he could ride his bicycle.

The time with his family passed too quickly for Kanda, and soon he was back to his basement room and his studies. He completed his thesis on time and passed it with a B. He also passed all his written and practical examinations with three As, four Bs, and a C. He had to return home soon after the examinations and could not stay for the graduation ceremony.

Kanda's one year in London was a very busy time, but he managed to make time to enjoy the London city life. He spent some time with his friend Bonny and also went out with school friends from Kenya and Ghana. He did not venture much out of London, and the only places he visited outside the city were Luton, some thirty miles out of London, and Brighton, which is close to fifty miles away. You love a place more when it is time to leave than when you first saw it.

During the 1988 December Christmas holiday, the students had to vacate the student hostel for five weeks, and a friend in his class, Nayab, from Pakistan offered Kanda his apartment for free for that whole period while he was away home for the holiday in Pakistan. Seven years later in 1996, Kanda and Nayab would have a surprise meeting in Pakistan, where both were attending a strategic management seminar sponsored by the British Commonwealth at the Lahore University of Management in the city of Lahore. Nayab was in his element, at home in his traditional attire, and he and Kanda recognized each other instantaneously across a room full of many other people. They updated each other on what had transpired since the time they left London. Both were working in the field of human resources, and Nayab was just starting a family. It was a very happy reunion and a renewal of an enduring friendship.

Lahore is a very beautiful city with lots of historical and cultural attractions. Its enchanting Old City, also referred to as the Walled City, is the cultural heart of Lahore. Kanda and the other international seminar participants enjoyed their stay at the Lahore University. For many of them, however, a whole period of five weeks of sobriety was a new experience! There were rumors though of the availability of liquor on the black market, but the rumors also came with a warning of severe consequences if caught. What Kanda and the other international participants did not know then, however, was that while alcohol was difficult to find, the Muslim ban on alcohol did not apply to non-Muslims and non-Pakistanis. Another new experience for most of the international participants was the spicy food. Even the food that was specially prepared for the international participants, which was supposedly mild, still tasted very spicy for some.

Kanda had arrived in Pakistan through Karachi and had a glimpse of the country's old capital city. He also had the opportunity to visit the beautiful city of Islamabad, Pakistan's new national capital city. Kanda fell in love with the marble architecture that is characteristic of the city. The Faisal Mosque was a wonder to behold. When its construction was completed in 1986, it was the largest in the whole world. Since then, however, there have been other larger ones, and it is now the fifth largest in the world but still remains the largest in South Asia. The Faisal Mosque is a monumental marvel that radiates a spiritual reverence that is overwhelming even among non-Muslims. Kanda's overall impression of Pakistan was of a country on a fast track from the old to the modern as exemplified by the sight of the latest car models side by side with a buffalo-drawn cart on the streets of Lahore.

Kanda left London to return to Zimbabwe on September 19, 1989. The following weekend, family and friends organized a small welcoming party. Kanda's Uncle Sam, the same one from the cave at the Market Square, became the joke of the day when in a speech welcoming Kanda back, he referred to the gathering as a farewell party as if Kanda was going away again. It felt good to be back home with family. It was also good to be back at work at the bank. A short while after his return, he was promoted to the position of assistant general manager, a position that came with many good benefits including a company car. Kanda was eager to start putting into practice some of the ideas and skills he got from his study in London. But there were some basic problems. Human resource planning can only be meaningful within the context of an overall organizational strategy. Unless an organization and everyone in it are clear about the organization's goals and the operating objectives, it becomes difficult to come up with meaningful decisions on, say, recruitment, training, compensation, and so on. The old notion in the bank at the time was that the life of a central bank was guaranteed by statute, and there was no need for some of the fancy stuff like strategic planning and corporate strategy. For any organization, however, lack of clarity about its goals and objectives results in distortions in human resources decisions, such as a compensation and retention policy that is misdirected. A practical example was when the bank invited a very well-respected former chief executive in the banking industry to help the bank come up with a human resources strategy for the Reserve Bank. Obviously, he had a bias for commercial banking, and he came up with this idea that banking was the core business of the Reserve Bank. He then recommended that all the employees from the clerical grade and above in all areas of the bank should study for the Institute of Bankers diploma. Financial incentives were put in place to support the new policy. Years later, when a formal strategic planning exercise was finally carried out, the bank came up with two goals: preserving the value of the domestic currency as its primary goal and the stability of the financial markets as a subsidiary goal, thus shifting the bank's whole focus from its commercial banking business to the economics function and the banking supervision function as its main operations. This kind of shift obviously comes with major implications for human resources decisions.

At the time Kanda came back to the bank, he tried to incorporate some of his ideas within the situation as it was. He had earlier on pointed out the importance of strategic planning, and this time, he became an outspoken advocate for it. The 1990 managers' conference presented Kanda the opportunity to show what he had learned during his study abroad. He presented the findings of his thesis, which concluded that future promotion expectations that arose from the current speed of promotions would far exceed the opportunities available to accommodate them in the near future. While the presentation generated a lot of interest among the conference attendees, his recommendation that the bank needed to be more circumspect with regard to future promotions in order to minimize future problems was not well-received by some who took it from a personal point of view. The recommendation to purposely slow down promotions courted the disfavor of some of the senior staff who were in a hurry to get to the top, a disfavor that would, in time, hamper Kanda's own advancement in the bank. One particular incident of lobbying against Kanda's advancement by one of the senior staff who was generally viewed as petty and small-minded is on record, in writing.

In 1993, Kanda's boss, who was now deputy general manager, passed away in a car accident. His death was a huge loss to the bank and to Kanda personally. Subsequently, Kanda was upgraded to replace him as deputy general manager and head of human resources. He could now feel the weight of his new responsibilities as the top authority on human resources issues in the bank. At that time, he was also studying for the master of business administration (MBA) degree on a part-time basis at the University of Zimbabwe, with the approval and financial support of the bank. While Kanda was content with the professional qualifications that he had for the job he was doing, he had always felt the need to understand the business world within which the Reserve Bank was operating as a major participant. The need for this knowledge background became more apparent as he moved up the ladder into the ranks of senior management of the bank.

The MBA study program proved to be more difficult than Kanda had anticipated. He had no free time at all because of the many home assignments he had to complete and the classes that he had to attend during weekend and holiday periods. It appeared as if the pressure on students was a deliberate component of the whole study program. It was hard to maintain a workable balance between school work, work demands at the bank, and family responsibilities. At home, he left his library room inside the house, preferring to use the workshop in the outbuilding for his study work, and the saying "Daddy is not to be disturbed" became a refrain in Kanda's family. The hard work was worth it though, and Kanda graduated with his MBA degree in 1995. His aging mother was able to attend and witness her son being capped at the graduation ceremony.

In 1997, Kanda played a major role in addressing some the problems he had predicted years earlier. The bank had become too bloated, with many employees now bunched up in grades with nowhere up to go. Following a formal strategic planning exercise, the bank embarked on a major restructuring exercise, which resulted in massive retrenchments that shook the bank and left many employees traumatized. Following the restructuring exercise, Kanda was reassigned to a newly created position of head of institutional development, with responsibilities for human resources policy and the bank's overall corporate strategy. In January 2001, he was appointed advisor in the governor's office. Among his duties were his meetings with the governor first thing every morning and also as and when needed to discuss any issues, especially human resource matters that impacted the well-being of the bank. For Kanda, this appointment as advisor to the governor was a position of honor in the last days of his service in the Reserve Bank of Zimbabwe.

In 2002, rumors started circulating that the ruling Zanu-PF party of Robert Mugabe was planning to bring in its own people to replace the senior staff of the bank and that the governor was going to be removed even before the end of his term. Kanda did not think that his future in the bank would be secure under this development. Pretty much everybody close to him in the bank knew he did not support Zanu-PF but the opposition, MDC (Movement for Democratic Change) party, which was led by Morgan Tsvangirai. There was a time when during the early years of the MDC party, it was okay to openly talk politics and political affiliations. Mugabe himself, at one point, had said he welcomed opposition parties as that would facilitate democracy in the country. So staff in the bank used to openly discuss their political views, especially during the lunch breaks in the staff canteen. But from the time the Zanu-PF government began losing popularity among the people, things had changed, and it was no longer safe to be known to belong to or to support opposition parties. At one time, Kanda was approached in private by one of the bank's senior security staff to advise him against disclosing his political views, saying that the government's Central Intelligence Organization (CIO) kept files on all senior management in the Reserve Bank of Zimbabwe and other government institutions and parastatals. It was thus clear that if the rumors were true, there would be no future for him in the bank. He discussed his case with his boss, the governor, and tendered his application for early retirement effective December 2002. As it turned out, this was one of Kanda's best decisions ever as everybody knows what happened to the Reserve Bank and the country's economy when Mugabe's people took over the running of the bank. The Reserve Bank became Zanu-PF's ATM machine and the official distributer of political patronage and freebees to Zanu-PF's allies and cronies to the detriment of the entire country to this day. The economy went into a tailspin, with Zimbabwe's inflation under the bank's stewardship peaking at about eighty billion percent month on month and ninety sextillion percent year on year in 2008! Zimbabwe became a nation of poor trillionaires, with businesses, savings, and pensions all wiped out. Professional central banking went with the bank management that Kanda is proud to have been part of.

For twenty years, the bank had become part of Kanda's life. The bank provided him with the opportunities to grow and flourish in his career and general well-being. It had fulfilled his yearning for furthering his education. It gave Kanda his first house in one of the best suburbs in the country as well as his first brand-new car. The bank also had an education assistance scheme that allowed Kanda to send his children to the best schools in the country, such as Hartmann House, Springvale, Watershed, and Peterhouse. At the time of Kanda's retirement, his daughter Kuda was studying medicine in America. Kanda and his family had enjoyed many wonderful holidays at the bank's holiday facilities at Nyanga and Kariba. His family's visit to him while at college in London is unforgettable. The bank's business travel exposed him to many other peoples and cultures within the region in Africa and abroad in Europe and Asia. Kanda gave the bank his best, and the bank, in turn, did the same for him.

Kanda and Rosemary at their wedding (1980)

Rosemary with the children at Trafalgar Square, London (1989)

Kanda's children back home with their bicycles from London (1989)

Kanda and Rosemary with children, from left to
right are Kuda, Mutsa, and Tatenda (2002)

The family home in Harare, Zimbabwe

KANDA LEAVES
FOR ENGLAND

Inexorably Westbound
What would Grandpa say
Should he have had a say

The Reserve Bank pension scheme was considered one of the best in the country, and Kanda left the bank with what was then a pretty good pension package of benefits, which included a third pension commutation, free medical aid coverage for life, and free access to the bank's holiday facilities at Nyanga and Kariba as well as free access to the bank's sports club facilities in Harare. He was also leaving with his company car paid for at book value. He, however, never intended to retire from the world of work. His plan was to look for a human resource consulting company he could join. Failing which, he could form his own consulting company. He had also been setting up some income-generating projects at his village. He had fenced his nine-acre plot at the village and built a ten thousand-liter water tank with underground piping to draw water from Nhora River some three hundred meters away. He had a T-35 truck and a tractor with a plough, harrow, and trailer. His plan was to grow a variety of farm produce for sale at markets in Harare and the nearby smaller towns of Shamva and Bindura. Kanda had also just finished building a hardware shop at the Rutope Business Center near his village to supply the villagers and many recently settled small farmers in the area with agricultural inputs and building materials.

While Kanda was attending to his plans at the village, he was also looking for consulting work in Harare, and on April 2, 2003, he signed his first consulting contract with Floraline (PVT) Limited, a flower growing company on Harare Drive in Harare. The contract was to supply human resources services at the rate of five thousand dollars an hour. Kanda considered the consulting fee quite reasonable for a first-time consulting contract. About a week or so later, however, something happened that would upend all of Kanda's plans in Harare and at the village.

For many years, Kanda's favorite drinking place was a small pub at the Kampfinza Hotel in nearby Kampfinza suburb. The hotel itself had ceased operating, but the pub at the back remained open with David, the regular barman. With almost the same people patronizing the pub for a long period, the general atmosphere in the pub resembled that of a club where everybody knew everybody else. Among the patrons was a young man named John (not his real name) who worked in the President's Office, a euphemism for the CIO. John was a very nice, well-educated, and well-spoken young man. He appeared to have been well-traveled and, according to him, had once been posted to Europe on his job. He was the type that easily made friends with people around him. He was aware as most of the patrons were that Kanda often traveled on business in the SADC (Southern African Development Community) region. One day he approached Kanda in private and asked that Kanda supply him with some information from his travels.

One of Kanda's roles while he was head of human resources and as head of institutional development in the Reserve Bank was to represent the bank on a forum of the SADC central banks that was tasked with the formulation and promotion of central bank training for the region's central banks. The forum met regularly in alternate member countries, and during that time, Kanda had traveled to South Africa, Swaziland, Namibia, Botswana, Mozambique, Malawi, Tanzania, and Kenya. While some of these countries had hosted several of the forum meetings, the forum kept deferring holding any meetings in Zimbabwe due to political instability and security concerns for the forum members. What John was asking for from Kanda was some kind of report on how the forum members and the people in general in the countries that Kanda visited viewed Zimbabwe. When Kanda consulted with his boss, it was strongly felt that the bank could not be seen to be spying on its regional colleagues or anybody else. It was suggested that Kanda could give the CIO man copies of the minutes of the forum meetings, and John went along with that idea. There was really nothing of particular interest for him in those minutes, except perhaps the constant refrain that meetings could not be held in Zimbabwe because of security concerns. So each time Kanda came back from one of his business trips, he would signal to John, and they would go out of the pub to his car, where Kanda would hand over the minutes to him. As time went on, however, John seemed to want the other patrons to know that he and Kanda were working together on something, and that made Kanda very uncomfortable.

Sometime in early April, a few months after Kanda had left the Reserve Bank, John and his friend (also a regular patron at the pub and of the same name as his) and Kanda were sitting at a table together. Kanda was on one side of the table, and the other two were on the other side. John then said to Kanda something to the effect that "Now that you are done with your honorable job at the Reserve Bank of Zimbabwe, the President's Office is very interested in your services, and you will be hearing from the President's Office in the next two weeks or so." Kanda was stunned, and his response was noncommittal. He did not stay long in the pub that day.

The CIO is the Zanu-PF's instrument of coercion and brutality. These are the state security agents that were and are still today blamed for the abductions, disappearances, rapes, torture, and killings of political opposition activists and journalists. People at work, family, friends, and neighbors all knew that Kanda was an active member of the MDC, which was in opposition to the Zanu-PF oppressive regime. The CIO and its work were anathema to Kanda. Apart from his politics, Kanda's Christian faith, and his social work training to help people ran counter to the work of the CIO as he understood it. For him to witness, let alone participate, in the CIO atrocities was unimaginable to Kanda. He was, however, also aware that once he was approached to work for the CIO, he would not be able to refuse and hope to be let alone.

After discussing his dilemma with family and friends, Kanda decided to disappear from the country for a while. When his daughter Kuda left for college in America in 2001, Kanda and his family obtained ten-year American visas in the hope of visiting her someday in the future. Kanda also had a five-year British visa, which he had intended to use to travel via London to visit his daughter now that he had the time to do so. On deciding where he could go, Kanda chose to flee to London because it was closer to home. This was all thought to be a short visit because at the time, there were high expectations for political change in the country. This was the time that the MDC was orchestrating what was deemed the final push to remove the Zanu-PF government from power. The final push was slated for the following months of June and July, and people really believed that some big change was going to happen. Kanda's plan was to return home as soon as the political situation had improved. In the meantime, he hoped to use his social work qualification to find some work in England. Britain had employed many social workers from Zimbabwe in the past.

Kanda put his business plans at the village on hold and recommended a fellow human resources practitioner, Morgan, to take over his newly signed human resources consulting contract. While he was making his preparations to leave, he was always fearful of being summoned to the President's Office as the time was getting close to the two weeks mentioned by John. He had since stopped going to the Kampfinza pub. Kanda finally left for London on April 27 before any further contact with John. Years later, John was said to have died by suicide, and his friend, the other John, was said to have moved to Botswana.

In the midst of all this drama with the CIO man, Kanda's family was dealing with another situation involving his son, Tatenda. Tatenda had had several scuffles with some Zanu-PF youths who accused him of not participating in their party activities, saying that he was too proud of himself because he went to a white school. He had just completed his form five at Peterhouse School in Marondera in December 2002 and was due to return for his form six in the new year. Because of the concern for his safety, the parents decided to withdraw him from school and send him to college in America, where his sister was already studying. He applied and was offered admission at the Lansing Community College in Lansing, Michigan's capital city. When he applied for the student visa, however, the application was denied. It was a difficult time for Tatenda and the family. The family finally decided that since Tatenda already had an American visitor's visa, he should just go to America in the hope that his sister and Kanda's friend, Charles, who was also there, would help him work out something for himself there. Charles was that friend of Kanda who had connected Kanda and his wife, Rosemary, years earlier in Kwekwe. He was one of the bridegroom's attendants at Kanda's and Rosemary's wedding. Charles had also played a major role in Kuda's decision to go to America for her college education, and he and a cousin of his named Joe had received and helped her settle down. The family was thus confident that Charles would be able to help Tatenda deal with the immigration requirements for him to stay and study in America.

In England, Kanda was going to stay with a cousin named Cami, the son of Msande and grandson of *Mbuyanhini*. Cami lived with his wife and their two young children in the city of Hull, some two hundred miles up north of London. Kanda was going to live with them while he looked for work to sustain himself. His final place to stay in England was going to be determined by where he was able to find work, with London as his main focus. When he got to London, he took the bus to Hull. He preferred the bus to the train so he could see more of the English countryside, and the trip took about eight hours with some stops on the way. Kanda thought Hull was a little nice city, and he was well-received by Cami and his family. Their little daughter, Tasha, took an immediate liking to the uncle from *kumusha* (home) and did not seem to mind being deprived of her bedroom.

One thing became very clear from the beginning, and that was that he would not be able to find a professional job as a social worker in England as he had hoped. It was pointed out from all his enquires that he could not be considered for such a job because he had been out of social work practice for too long. There were, however, opportunities to update his social work qualification with some short study courses. As he was not planning for any long-term employment in

England, he did not think it worthwhile spending the time and money upgrading his qualifications. For now, he was looking for any type of work available and thus began his engagement in general labor jobs. He worked in a bottling company and several food packing factories. The place he worked the longest during his stay in Hull was a frozen potato packing factory in Bridlington, some twenty miles north of Hull. The work was carried out in conditions under below freezing temperature. In the summer time, the workers brought extra warm clothes to put on as they got into the factory and would take them off when they went out during break times. One had to get used to the constant change from extreme heat to extreme cold and vice versa. In Zimbabwe, Kanda was used to seeing white women working in offices and other soft occupations only and never laboring in factories. Here, there were white young women toiling and heaving heavy loads of sacks of potatoes alongside the men. It was, at times, even hard to keep up with their pace of work.

Each time Kanda hears the song "Where Is the Love?" by the Black Eyed Peas, his mind is thrown back to the time that he and the other factory workers were traveling through the English countryside on their way from Hull to Bridlington. The song played almost every morning on the van that transported them to and from the factory. The countryside always looked beautiful, serene in the morning mist with small English cottages dotted here and there on the open landscape. One day, Kanda did not use the regular transport to work, preferring a ride in the private car of one of the workers, a white South African young man of Afrikaner background. At some point as they drove through the countryside, the young man asked Kanda what the place they were passing through reminded him of. Kanda looked around but could not see anything that would remind him of anything, and he told him so. The young man laughed and asked Kanda if he could smell anything. He did not have to say anything more! Kanda quickly understood what the young man, who must have grown up on a farm, was experiencing; that musty smell of cow dung in the morning mist that Kanda had lived with at the village and the farm.

About a month after Kanda left Zimbabwe, his wife started receiving phone calls from people who did not want to identify themselves. One persistent caller said he was a friend of Kanda's but would not say his name. When Kanda's wife told them that he had left the country on a short visit abroad, they did not seem to believe it. Then one morning a few weeks later, there was some graffiti outside on the electric gate with "SELL OUT" scrawled across the gate in red crayon. This was really frightening for Kanda's wife, who was living alone with two domestic workers. Their last daughter, Mutsa, was at boarding school at Peterhouse, and Kanda's other daughter Cynthia had gotten married in 2002 and was now living away with her husband. There were other suspicious and disturbing incidents, which clearly indicated that this could not have been some random mischief by some people in the neighborhood. The family believed all those incidents were linked to the reason why Kanda had left the country. The family did not think that it would be of any help to go to the police with this type of a case. It was (and still is) quite common that people who reported politically related cases to the police ended up being in trouble themselves in the hands of the police who should be helping and protecting them.

After discussing this situation with Kanda in England and other family members in Harare, Rosemary left the family house and went to stay with her sister Eleanor and her husband in the Hatfield suburb while considering what to do next. Kanda decided that Rosemary and Mutsa should come and join him in England, and they would then work out something together. Kanda had managed to rent a municipal flat on Constable Street in Hull in preparation for the family's coming. Rosemary already had a British visa, but Mutsa's application for a visa to England was denied. The only other option to leave the country was to go to America as both Rosemary and Mutsa already had American visas. There were extensive telephone discussions between Kanda in England, his wife in Harare, Kuda, and Kanda's friend Charles in Michigan. What was happening to Kanda's family was how many Zimbabwean families were now living, strewn apart all over the world, fleeing from their homeland, just because someone wanted to remain in power and eat alone. As all this was going on in the Kanda family, the political momentum for the final push by the MDC appeared to be dissipating. This was now June, and there were no significant developments on the issue with no indication that there would be anything different in the coming month. The whole country was clearly in a state of despair. Kanda's family finally decided that the best thing for the family was for Rosemary and Mutsa to go and join Kuda and Tatenda in America and that, circumstances permitting, Kanda would also join them there so that the family could be together again.

Rosemary withdrew Mutsa from school, put the house on the market for rent, and distributed the household items to extended family members; some of the items for them to use and other bigger and valuable ones for safekeeping. There was no guarantee that the family would be allowed to stay in America beyond the visiting period normally allowed, and so the family did not want to dispose of their belongings at this stage. Rosemary and Mutsa boarded the flight to America on June 30, 2003.

The Kanda family was now at a crossroads, unclear where their circumstances would lead to. When people leave their home for an indefinite time, there are many things, property and otherwise, that need to be taken care of for the time they would be away. There would be no time for Kanda to go back to Zimbabwe to sort out some of those things. The most important thing to him then was his family's safety and well-being. The family was received and accommodated by Charles and his wife, Jane, in Lansing, Michigan, and Kanda would join them three months later.

Kanda's circumstances were clear that he would, for an indefinite time, be separated from a large part of his family: from his daughter Cynthia and her family, from his mother at the village, and from his brothers and sisters and the rest of the extended family. From the time Kanda left Kwekwe and Masvingo to come to Harare, he had kept close contact with his family and relatives. Kanda never forgot his roots and the village that brought him up and encouraged him to go to school. He was a regular visitor at the village, where he and his brothers had built their mother a beautiful four-bedroom house with a solar system. Like his father before him, Kanda was always available to offer assistance to his people at the village. There was a time that he won a Reserve Bank of Zimbabwe's old bullion truck in a raffle, and for several years, he sent his driver and the truck to help the villagers carry their harvests to the market free of charge. He also used his tractor to plough for free the crop fields of two elderly widows and a special needs couple at the village. He also extended this free service to the head of the village in honor of his position as guardian of the village. For the rest of the villagers, all they needed to do was to supply the diesel needed for the tractor to cover the acreage they wanted ploughed. Kanda also made available to the village his cars in times of illness and death. With Kanda now not returning to Zimbabwe for quite a while, the village was definitely going to feel his absence.

Kanda with Tasha (2003)

KANDA IS HEADED TO AMERICA

America, the great paradox
Of its apparent greatness and goodness
Of the evil at its very core
Who be the arbiter

Kanda had gone to England for what he had hoped would be a few months. He ended up being in that country for over five months. The much-hoped for political change in Zimbabwe never happened, and his family had fled home to America. He had been well taken care of in Hull by his cousin and his wife, Gertrude, an excellent cook. He had enjoyed the companionship of their daughter, Tasha, and Cami's young brother, Lloyd, who was also living and working in Hull. When he later reflected back to his time in Hull, he realized that he had a debt to settle. One day soon after his arrival in Hull he, Cami and Tasha were at a gas station, and Tasha asked Kanda, "Uncle, can you buy me some Pringles?" Kanda had no idea what pringles were, and when he looked to Cami for some enlightenment, all Cami said was "Not now, Tasha." The incident passed, and Kanda forgot about it, even after he later got to know what Pringles were. On looking back now, however, the idea that the uncle who displaced his niece from her room for months, with not a complaint from her, could not buy her a small can of Pringles she asked for, which cost less than two dollars, has made Kanda feel bad about himself. He has vowed that the next time he saw Tasha, who has since grown up and now a college graduate, he would buy her a can of Pringles! He has also been keen to see Tasha's brother, who was a baby then but now very tall like his grandfather, Msande. Tasha has also since had another young brother named Jayden.

Kanda left his host family in Hull for America on October 3, 2003, and was received by his family and Charles at the Detroit airport. It is hard to try and sum up a full and complete impression of America. To attempt to describe America is to be reminded of the famous Indian parable of the three blind men and the elephant. One variation of the parable is that one blind man touches the side of the huge animal and says an elephant is like a brick wall, the second touches the trunk and says the elephant is like a snake, and the third touches the leg and says the elephant is like a great trunk of a tree. Each of the three men thinks he is right and the others are wrong. The elephant is all those things plus more and big. That is one way to look at America. It is all kinds of many things and in a big way.

One stark view of America is the extent to which it has gone to delink itself from its colonial parent, Britain. It has, however, never been clear to Kanda whether the differences between America and Britain were the result of a deliberate plan or whether all or some of them are by mere chance or are a poor imitation of the original. Take, for instance, the English language. There is now a clear distinction between the original Queen's English language and the American version. If you take words like check for cheque, labor for labour, color for colour, program for programme, etc., were these changes deliberate or could they have been some misspellings by some unlettered pioneer that were then incorporated into the local vocabulary? Then you have some weird expressions such as "different than" instead of "different from." There also appears to be no present past tense in the American English version, and Kanda has heard people say "I am going to have my hair did" or "I have went!" English, really! This bastardized English language, like most things in America, has become big and bigger than the original Queen's language. When you try and use the original spellings on most computer software, they would be rejected in favor of the American version. The muted call to make the bastardized American version the official English language worldwide displays the audacity and unbridled arrogance of a superpower. The observation about the differences in the English language also applies to many other things, such as driving on the right instead of the left side of the road, flipping the switch up instead of down to turn on electricity, and so on.

America is among the most developed countries in the world, with some of the most educated, yet it also has some of the most ignorant people compared to other countries, even among the least developed. Many Americans only know of their country and very little about elsewhere in the world. There are people who have gone to school who will ask who the president of Africa is as if Africa is one country like America. Kanda was once asked, "How did you get to America? Did you drive?" There have been many situations when Kanda would tell someone that he is from Zimbabwe, and that person would say something like, "Oh, I used to have a friend so and so from Ghana. Do you know him?" As if Africa is some small village where everybody knows everybody else. There are Americans in today's world who think that in Africa, there are wild animals roaming the countryside everywhere, unaware that people have to visit game reserves to see the wild animals. The ignorance about the greater world and its geography and history, even from some people who should know better, is astounding.

America is well-known for its worst evil to humanity, slavery, but it also has some of the nicest and most generous people on earth. For many of these people, that goodness derives from religious and other philosophical considerations, while for many others, it's simply inherent humanity. When Kanda's family arrived in America, it was received with this goodness and generosity in unmeasurable ways. When Kuda first came to America in 2001, she looked for a church with similar practice to the Methodist Church she was used to back home. She could not find what she was looking for among the African American churches. At one African American church she visited, it was like all the church members were in for a dressing fashion competition, and the congregation also appeared to be preoccupied with the status of their pastor compared to the other church pastors in terms of the latest car make and model he was driving, whether or not he lived in White Hills, and whether or not he had a private jet, rather than focusing on the gospel. Kuda's search ended up at a small congregation by the name Faith Church, which was headed by Pastor Joel. The congregation was mostly white, with the exception of one black family from Liberia and a few other blacks who occasionally attended. When some of the church members heard about Kuda's family coming to America, they were ready for them. One couple in particular virtually adopted the family. The family was taken to the Burlington store to get winter coats of their choice. They were given a bed and some bedding, some bicycles, laptops, stationery, and other smaller things. When Kanda joined the family in Michigan, they were invited to outings and meals. Sometime later, another couple gave the family their seven-seater Pontiac van for free. The van came fully serviced with new tires and all its previous service records. On another occasion, one member of the church, a very nice elderly man whom Kanda's family secretly adopted as their uncle in America, quietly slipped a one hundred-dollar bill in Kuda's palm as the congregation was leaving the church. There was enormous goodwill toward the family from the pastor and the rest of the congregation. This kind of goodwill and generosity for an immigrant, especially one from a poor country coming to America with only a suitcase and a few dollars to themselves, is unmeasurable. Just the feeling of being accepted and loved goes a long way to make less severe the anxiety and hardships of finding one's way around in a foreign land.

These were some of Kanda's early impressions of America. He also had some general visual impression of the country as they drove from Detroit airport the day he arrived. Some of the houses in the neighborhoods that they passed alongside the highway were no better than some of the not-so-good parts of Mbare in Harare. At some point during the drive, Kanda thought their car had a puncture, only to realize that the bumps and jolts were due to the uneven surface on the road. Coming from a third-world country with lots of potholes on the roads, Kanda had assumed that in America, it's always all smooth driving. America is indeed many things, and there was more yet to see and experience.

When Kanda joined the family in Lansing, Kuda's housemate, another student from Zimbabwe, moved out to leave room for Kuda's family in the two-bedroom apartment they had shared. The family moved from Charles's house to the apartment. The apartment was meant to be student accommodation, and with Kanda's family of five, it was clearly overcrowded and against the provisions of the lease agreement. Whenever there was a knock at the door, some members of the family would disappear in the bedrooms for fear the landlord might not approve the overcrowding.

The first days, weeks, and months were tough and full of uncertainty and anxiety. The financial situation was tight. Kanda had saved some few hundred pounds in England, and Kuda was studying and working part-time as well. Fortunately, Tatenda and Mutsa were able to continue with their high school studies free of charge. With time, Kanda and Rosemary were able to find some odd jobs here and there while they waited for formal authorization to work in America. Kanda benefited a great deal from one fellow Zimbabwean who had been in America for many years. Peter (not his real name) helped many students and other newly arrived Zimbabweans with some piece work that sustained them during their early days in Lansing. Peter bought depressed houses for remodeling and resale. For many months, that was the work Kanda did for Peter, clearing and cleaning up dirty properties, demolishing and rebuilding dry walls, patching up floors, laying on carpeting, painting, and so on. It was hard work, but it helped to keep the family afloat.

While Peter might have been benefiting from some cheap labor, his assistance to many new arrivals from Zimbabwe was quite significant because generally, Zimbabweans in the diaspora were not known to be very helpful to new arrivals from home unless it was family or a close friend. Unlike many other diasporans from other parts of Africa, who rallied together to offer assistance to new arrivals from their countries, there was no such collective sense of responsibility among the Zimbabweans. Kanda's experience in England and America was that there was more competition than cooperation among the Zimbabweans in the diaspora. Many other Africans had national associations and came together to commemorate important national events such as independence days, but there was not much of that among the Zimbabweans in the diaspora. Instead, there were cases in which some Zimbabweans were said to have gone to the immigration authorities to report on fellow Zimbabweans who were suspected of living illegally in a foreign country. Instead of celebrating one another's successes, the tendency was to pull them down. This reminded Kanda of his people's folklore about what some people have called the witchcraft syndrome. In times past, if someone in the village produced an exceptionally good crop compared to all the others, he was accused of witchcraft, that he had a *divisi*, a potent juju that sucked the plant food from other people's crop fields to feed his own. So instead of praising the good farmer and learning from him, they sought to pull him down. The situation of the Zimbabweans in the diaspora was worsened by the toxic and polarizing politics back home. At one time, Kanda and a group of other Zimbabweans in Indiana tried to form a Zimbabwe association that would bring Zimbabweans together for social and other purposes, but their efforts were scuttled by the presence of some people who were suspected of being Zimbabwe government's CIO agents. The only thing to survive from that effort was a burial society, which still exists to date. In fact, the only thing that is sure to bring Zimbabweans together is death. The only large gatherings of Zimbabweans in the diaspora that Kanda has witnessed have been at funerals. Zimbabweans do come together when one of them dies, and they are generous in contributing money to send the body back home, even when they did not care about the deceased when alive. On the whole, Kanda believes that the witchcraft syndrome and the attendant "pull him down" mentality (PHD syndrome) are why Zimbabwe, and perhaps all of Africa, are where they are today compared to the other countries of the world.

The irony of being an immigrant in America from a poor country is that once you get to America and while you are busy struggling to survive, people back home believe you are already awash with the United States dollars, and they start to tell you their financial problems! People back home have no conception of what it takes to survive and establish oneself in a foreign country where one comes to with nothing to help them kick-start a new life. The Kanda family was, however, lucky to have friends like Charles and Jane and new friends from church. Charles advanced Kanda a car for the family to use and only pay for it later when he started working. Charles had done the same for Tatenda on his arrival. The Kanda family also received considerate assistance from the Catholic Charities organization, where Kanda had also had a stint as a volunteer at their refugee center.

Rosemary was the first in the family to obtain work authorization in April 2004. She got a job at a factory that employed mostly recent immigrants, a significant transition from her executive marketing job back home with staff below her, an office, and a company car. The family was, however, grateful that she had a job, and she became the sole family breadwinner until Kanda also got his work authorization later that September. Things were now beginning to shape up for the family, and they were able to move out of the small apartment into a regular three-bedroom rental one.

Kanda's preferred choice of work was in the areas of social work and human resources management. His many attempts to find work in the human resources field were fruitless. It felt like this field of work was difficult to break through for foreigners. He could also not hope to get a professional social work job with his three-year university diploma in social work. Most professional social work jobs in America required at least a master's degree in social work or related field. However, almost all the various lower-level jobs that Kanda then did in America were social work related. It was the type of work that took you into the belly of the American world, far removed from the glamor and glitter above, a world of the disadvantaged, the poor, the sick, the homeless, and the forgotten. His first job was as a youth counselor at a home for emotionally troubled children. These were children who had been in various childcare situations, including juvenile detention and failed foster care and adoption. The job was a real challenge, but with moments of rewarding experiences as well. The children could engage in extreme negative behaviors toward the other children and the staff. The difficulty for a counselor was to appreciate that the negative behavior directed at him was not about him, the counselor, but about the person exhibiting it, someone trying to deal with his or her own demons, so to speak. Kanda always tried to respond to a child acting out with a sympathetic demeanor and attitude in an attempt to pacify and disarm the child rather than emphasize correction and discipline. This worked at times but did not at other times. During his one year as youth counselor, Kanda had established some meaningful and therapeutic relationships with some of the children. One of the bigger children, a black boy, became a defender and protector of Kanda from the negative behavior of the other children. For one small black girl, Kanda reminded her of her grandfather, and she became very close to him. She made Kanda a parting gift of a beautiful little doll at the time that he left the home. He also got a big surprise from another small white boy who generally kept much to himself. The boy gave Kanda his most favorite monkey toy, and on the day that Kanda left the home, the boy was at the door to check and make sure that Kanda had not left the gift behind. At the time that Kanda left the organization, there had been many children who had become closely attached to him in a manner that facilitated positive counseling, and it was sad to leave. The only reason Kanda left the home was because he had been offered a bigger and better-paying job elsewhere. One of Kanda's satisfying moments at the home for the children was his work with one of the senior children, a white girl. This was an intelligent and beautiful teen of sixteen years old, who was notorious for absconding from custody and indulging in all manner of misbehavior while out there in the community. At first, she did not want to talk with Kanda about her situation, but with encouragement, she opened up a little bit by bit. Kanda discovered that she was interested in writing short stories and poems and that she was actually very good at it. Kanda encouraged her to keep a diary and suggested that someday she might be able to write a book about her life experiences in the child welfare system, which might be useful to some future children in situations similar to her current one. She played that down, saying that she was a very bad person and that nothing good could ever come out of her. Kanda countered by saying that deep down in her heart, she was an angel, a *malaika* in Swahili. From then on, Kanda started calling her *malaika*. This must have touched her somehow, and she became very responsive to Kanda. In their ongoing interaction, she insisted that it was Kanda and not her who was the real *malaika*, and she then went on to write a poem for Kanda titled "*Malaika*." Kanda made a copy of the document for the file at the home and kept the original for inspiration and validation of his efforts to be of service to fellow human beings. The poem, in full, was as follows:

TO TIM
FROM (her name)

Malaika

Malaika is an angel
From God up above
Malaika is an angel
That brings you love
Malaika tries to do what is right
never do what is wrong
Malaika is the light
that is never gone
Malaika never gets mad
at God's children
he only gets sad
When he deals with bad children
Malaika makes me feel bad
Because when he tries to help
they make him look bad
because they don't know how he felt
Malaika is an angel
transformed into a man
Malaika knows he will
Malaika knows he can
Malaika does what he has to do
Malaika knows and will always love you
Your secrets Malaika knows
the way God goes Malaika will show
Malaika is an angel from God up above
Malaika is an angel
that brings you love

Kanda's second job in America was with an organization that catered for homeless people. He was an advocate for the homeless at their overnight shelter and longer-term transitional housing facility. When one is new in America, there is some dissonance in seeing a poor person in a country that is so advanced and so rich. In most third-world countries, a poor person is commonplace. In fact, in some of these countries, the poor are the majority and the well-to-do a tiny minority so that being poor is the norm rather than the exception. And in many of these countries, poverty does not necessarily result in homelessness because of extended family and other social systems that serve as safety nets for the unfortunate of society. As these social systems disintegrate, however, as is now happening in many developing countries, the problems of poverty and homelessness begin to mirror those of the developed countries, but with the disadvantage of not having sufficient financial and other resources to mitigate against them. Homelessness in America is, however, more than just poverty. It is a complex phenomenon of an interplay of many other factors, such as shortage of low-income housing, unemployment, mental illness and substance abuse, and the lack of the needed services for the last two. Substance abuse and mental illness appear to have a more enduring impact on homelessness than the other factors. The guests at the homeless shelter came from all different kinds of background and with different problems and needs, some of which were simple and straightforward and others more complex.

Kanda's job was to process the guests' intake and orientation to the shelter and the longer-term transitional housing. He set and monitored guests' daily and weekly goals. He facilitated the guests' access to other complementary services in the community, such as employment, health, transportation, personal documentation, and so on. He also provided some counseling and conflict resolution and problem solving as needed and compiled statistical records and reports for internal as well as external use. Because the guests could only stay at the shelter for periods of up to two weeks only at a time, with a certain interval of time before they could be accepted back, Kanda had the opportunity to meet many homeless people from all walks of life. It is amazing how much one can learn from and be inspired by people who may themselves be in some state of deprivation and want. The human mind and soul have a way of being their own even in the most dire of circumstances.

Kanda left his work with the homeless with another validation for his service to others. In October 2005, one man who had passed through the shelter as a guest wrote back to the organization as follows: "i want to take this time to thank you all for your kindness at the (name of the organization.) You are all remarkable people. I want to especially thank tim. he is a heck of a guy and very dedicated to what he does. he is the definition of what (name of organization) represents." Kanda's boss added to the message, "Good work, Tim!"

Kanda enjoyed his job at the homeless shelter but had to leave when his family decided to relocate, fleeing from the extreme cold and snow of the north to the warmer south in Indiana. Only Kuda, who was attending the Michigan State University, remained in Lansing. Kanda's first job in Indiana was with a state agency as a public assistance caseworker, assisting the needy with certain benefits. In Kanda's view, the public assistance processing approach was more mechanical, using a complex computer program to calculate the benefits, and was less the traditional one-on-one casework sessions that seek to understand the underlying causes of distress in order to come up with both immediate relief and longer-term remedy. It took Kanda quite a while to be conversant with the computer operating system. On the whole, he did not find much joy in this job and left after a year to take up a new job as a social worker in a nursing home.

There are thousands of nursing homes in America, and they, like most other services, range from the basic low-income to the elite. The one Kanda worked for was at the lower end of that spectrum. A nursing home environment is generally not a very pleasant one with all the old and sickly people. Some of the inmates are in states of hopelessness, which require complete intimate care all the time. With many of them in diapers, there is always some odor hanging in the air in some parts of the home. With all this, however, Kanda saw some of the most dedicated staff he had ever witnessed. Kanda's job was to assess and review the residents' psychosocial needs and problems and contribute to the development of the plans for their care, provide counseling and conflict resolution among the residents, facilitate residents' access to community resources and services, help residents remain connected to their families, and help those being discharged to minimize any problems of reentry to community. Some of the problems in Kanda's job were about residents who had kind of given up on life or were experiencing cognitive decline, which made any meaningful participation in their treatment plans difficult. Another of Kanda's tasks was the keeping and updating of residents' records in readiness for the regular state inspections. Kanda learned that for most nursing homes, these inspections and the potential penalties for noncompliance with state requirements were a source of constant fear, which led the homes to go to great lengths to hide mistakes and errors and engage in many otherwise unprofessional conduct in order to survive.

With six months in his job, there was a change of management. The new head was rumored to be keen on bringing some of the staff he had in his previous organization. The situation changed with the new head and was compounded by Kanda's supervisor, who was somehow insecure in her job, believing that Kanda had been brought in to eventually replace her. Although the supervisor did not have any academic qualifications for the job, she was quite competent in her job from many years of experience. The job of social work in a nursing home was completely new to Kanda, and he could not comprehend how he could be viewed as a threat to the supervisor. Anyway, the work situation became very unfavorable, and he left the nursing home.

Kanda later joined a charitable organization that catered to people with disabilities. He worked with adults in a group home setting with the primary responsibility of helping them to be more independent in their daily life activities. He worked with these special needs people for four years before he decided to leave full-time work, scaling down to part-time work as a companion for seniors in their homes. This was a job where one got into people's private homes, where one met people from all walks of life, the poor and the rich, the Christian and non-Christian, the Republican and the Democrat, the friendly and the unfriendly. One gets to know who prefers CNN, MSNBC, or Fox News and which of the channels never ever to tune in in their presence! Some would treat you like a friend and others like a housemaid. Some of the people would engage you in some way, while others would have nothing at all to do with you, although the family might have decided that that help was needed. It is a job where you see a people and a country from another angle.

Three years after landing in America, Kanda and his family moved into their brand-new home in one of America's upmarket suburbs. Kanda and Rosemary had picked a plot and a model of the house they wanted in a new subdivision of Noblesville, Indiana, and the developer then built the house for them from the bare ground up to the final two-story home. The family moved in in October 2006. The Kanda family could now smell a whiff of the American dream! America was now truly a home away from home, and it was here that the family would live for the next ten years. While Kanda worked to keep the ship afloat, all the other members of the family were also working and at the same time doing other things to improve their lives. Rosemary studied and completed her associate degree as a registered nurse. Tatenda completed his business studies degree at the Kelley School of Business, one of the top ranked business schools in the country. Mutsa completed her bachelor's and master's degrees and was now studying for her doctorate degree in international psychology. It was also the same period that Kuda completed her medical studies, got married to Charles Kunaka, and had their first child, a boy named Tanaka.

Kanda had two older grandchildren in Zimbabwe, Cynthia's children, Emmanuel, born 2003, and Rumbidzai, born 2005. But Tanaka was his first grandchild in America and the first for Rosemary. The child who had held the position of grandchild to Kanda in America was Chibu, the daughter of Sinikiwe, who was the daughter of Rosemary's older sister, Christina. Chibu was a nickname that Kanda preferred, and her real name was Thandiwe, named after her paternal grandmother. Chibu was the first child ever to call Kanda grandpa. It started from when she learned to speak by calling him kulu or *sekuru* for grandfather. There is something about being a grandfather, the pleasure of being recognized and being treated as such. Chibu was the first to do that for Kanda, and she will always have a special place in his heart.

Tanaka was born in July 2014, and he came with his own story. He was born on a Tuesday, and the following Saturday, Kanda and Rosemary drove to Michigan to see him. Their plan was to sleep over and return to Indiana the following Sunday. Kanda was very unhappy to hear that Kuda and Charles were due to go to work on Monday, leaving the baby with a babysitter. Kanda did not like the idea that his grandson would be left with a complete stranger beginning from that tender age. He discussed this with his wife and wondered if he could stay behind and take care of his grandson for at least a week while the parents went to work. The first problem was that he would not know how to feed the baby or to change the diapers. And what would he do if the baby started crying while alone with him? The second problem was that he too was due for work on Monday, and he was not sure that his employer would agree to give him some time off. His problem regarding time off was easily sorted out. Kanda called his supervisor and explained that he had a family crisis without going into details, and he was allowed one week off. The second step was to convince himself, his wife, and the child's parents that he could safely take care of the baby while the parents went to work. There were doubts everywhere. In Zimbabwe, taking care of babies is a woman's job. It would be frowned upon for a man to be seen feeding a baby and utterly unthinkable to be seen changing a diaper. This was a woman's job, and for those who could afford to employ help, this was the job of a maid. This was why Kanda had never played such a role with any of his children as they grew up. The family always had maids to take care of the children. Anyway, it was finally agreed that Kanda would stay behind and take care of his grandson for a week. His wife showed him how to change the diaper, and Kuda gave instructions on feeding the baby. The first day he was left with the baby, he was in a panic mode, ready to call his wife or the baby's mother at the slightest sign of a problem, but the day passed very well without any issues. He fed the baby and changed the diaper, and the baby slept most of the time. The second day was the same, and so was the next, and by the end of the week, he had become quite adept at manipulating and fitting the tiny diapers. The week that he stayed with the child allowed the parents some time to make other family arrangements for the baby's care. The week that followed, Rosemary's young sister, Eleanor, came from Indiana to babysit, and for the two weeks after that, Rosemary's cousin named Constance, also from Indiana, took care of the baby. By the end of that period, everybody felt that it was now okay to leave the baby with some other paid babysitter. Kanda looks back with pride that he broke with custom and did what he had to do for his grandson. It is not many grandparents, at least from home in Zimbabwe, who ever have that privilege.

It was during this period in Indiana that Kanda got hooked to American football. The Pistons basketball team had already introduced Kanda to the game of basketball in Michigan. Their win in the NBA finals in 2004 sealed Kanda's love for the game, which he had before then derisively viewed as a game of net ball that was played by men instead of women. Before he came to America, he had no interest in American football, a misnomer for a game that is played by hand by all of a team with the exception of one kicker! Calling a handball game football and relegating the real football game to some other name shows the eccentricity of the American mind at its height! Kanda thought it absurd calling the game football, but he, nevertheless, warmed up to it and began to understand the intricacies of the game in the buildup to the super bowl in 2007 when the Indiana Colts beat the Chicago Bears. Kanda was brought up on soccer, but he now enjoys American football more than soccer, which now appears to be slow and rather dull in comparison.

It was also during this period in Indiana that Kanda and his family were able to go back to visit Zimbabwe in 2012, almost ten years since they had left the country. It was a highly emotional time reuniting with Kanda's ninety-one-year-old mother, with Cynthia and her family, other family members, relatives, and friends. So much had happened in the interval, with many new family additions as well as many loved ones who had passed on. From then on, Kanda would spend most of his Christmas holidays with his mother, who passed on in 2019 at the age of ninety-eight. The family has continued to maintain close relations with the extended family back home.

Kanda witnessed one of America's major historic events during this period in Indiana, the election of an African of Kenyan origin as president of the United States of America. In Kanda's tradition and custom, a person's identity is defined by their father's lineage. From his little understanding of the American history, this election was seismic, an earth-shattering event. And what made it so significant for Kanda was that he was not just a witness but an active participant in making it happen. His very first vote in America elected a fellow African to the highest seat in America and the world. He had been surprised and disappointed by some of his fellow African Americans who had derided and tried to discourage Barrack Obama, saying that his audacious bid for the presidency would interfere with the smooth success of their anointed, Secretary Hillary Clinton. Obama's campaign was one of hope, and his election affirmed that even in the midst of dark times, hope and faith can prevail. The year 2020 presented Kanda with another opportunity to participate in a similar epic event, the election of the first woman, an African American, to the position of vice president of the United States of America. It is said that mankind originated in Africa, and the political developments in America were beginning to feel like the world was now inexorably on the path to return to its roots, the Motherland! This time Kanda became active in the Democratic campaign early, submitting his name to volunteer in the campaign. At one point, he got so concerned about the way the campaign was going, and he wrote to the chairman of the Biden campaign, with copy to the former president, Barrack Obama. The letter dated May 31, 2020, was as follows:

Dallas, Texas
May 31, 2020

The Chairman
The Biden Campaign
CC: President Obama
Dear Sir

I am very concerned about the lack of energy and inspiration in the Biden Campaign.

Right now, the nation is faced with two pressing issues: the coronavirus pandemic and the festering wound of racism as exemplified by the recent deaths of George Floyd, Ahmaud Arbery and Breonna Taylor. Both these issues are crying for national leadership. Trump's failure to lead on these issues presents Biden with a great opportunity to step in and provide the needed leadership even before he is elected president in November.

Of all the major issues facing America and the world: the current pandemic, climate change, health care, immigration, the economy, racism—this last one, racism, presents the greatest potential for any present or future president to build a long-lasting legacy at the level of Lincoln's Emancipation Declaration of 1863 and Johnson's Civil Rights Act of 1964.

Another major concern is that there is no visible energy and action in the Biden campaign. People are beginning to have the impression of a tired old man hiding behind the pandemic, just waiting and expecting to be elected president in November! We all know from the recent past what can happen from overconfidence and a sense of inevitability, even when clearly supported by the polls. We do see every day how desperate Trump is to win reelection but we do not see a corresponding level of urgency, energy and action in the Biden campaign. We need Biden in our face every day on tv, video, Twitter, Facebook and everywhere the same way Trump is. If he is not up to it, maybe its time he chooses his running mate now rather than later in order to inject the level of energy badly needed in the campaign.

What is the Biden campaign for? Great leaders are born of great visions. An aspiring leader cannot base their agenda on merely protecting or extending a predecessor's legacy and, extraordinary times call for extraordinary vision and action. We want Joe Biden "to go up the mountaintop" and tell us and the nation what he sees ahead for us and how he is going to get us there! Even if such vision is never fully realized as with King's 'I have a dream," still people need something uplifting, something to anchor their hopes on.

I am a Democrat through and through and will do whatever I can to see that Joe Biden is our next President. So, let's get to work!

Regards,

Timothy Majero

Kanda did not receive any response or acknowledgement from either the campaign or the former president, but as the campaign progressed, however, he was happy to see some improvements along the lines that he, and perhaps many others, had pointed out to the campaign. In November, Kanda voted and contributed to the win by Joe Biden and Kamala Harris. Kamala Harris becomes the first female and first triple-A (African, Asian, American) vice president with real potential to becoming the first female and first triple-A president.

America is regarded as the greatest democracy in the world. Once in a while, however, this great American democratic experiment does stumble. In the year 2020, Donald Trump reduced America to a tinpot banana republic by his refusal to concede his election loss even as he was clearly unwilling or unable to govern and protect the American people from the ravaging coronavirus pandemic. This bizarre episode was still ongoing at the time of telling this story.

Family home in Indiana, USA

From left: Cynthia, Sinikiwe, Kuda, and Mutsa at Kuda's wedding (2018)

Tatenda with Kuda at her wedding (2018)

Kanda with Chibu, the first child to call Kanda "Grandpa"

Kanda's grandson Tanaka wearing Grandpa's cap

America's Original Sin

Where do you turn to
When the defender of liberty denies you liberty
When the "We the people" is not you
Even the priest, the man of the cloth
Commands that you obey the massa

Kanda's story in America could never be complete without his views on what has been called America's original sin, the genocide of America's indigenous people and the enslavement of the African people, the twin evils upon which America was founded. Coming from Africa, slavery and its tendrils stretching all the way to the present times is personal to Kanda. He finds it painful to imagine the plight of the African slaves. You are abducted in your country in Africa, chained, and ripped away from your home and family, never to ever see them again. You are dragged across the ocean for months under the most inhuman conditions in a slave ship. In America, you are sold on the auction block like cattle to a white master, for whom you must toil from dawn to dusk all the days of your life with no compensation and no recourse to anyone or anywhere for relief or redress. You are stripped of your name and your identity and never to be regarded as a human being but massa's property. You have no recourse even to the founding fathers and their lofty ideals of "all men are created equal" and "one nation under God, with liberty and justice for all," for they too are complicit in the evil act. You are cold, starved, and regularly whipped and lynched for the most frivolous of infractions. If you are a woman, you can expect some of the worst abuses a woman can be subjected to. Should you manage to have a family, your spouse and children can be ripped away from you at massa's will and be sold away and never to see them again. In your old age, when the massa has exhausted your usefulness to him, you are discarded with no support to fall back on in the last days of your life on earth.

This is the plight of the African slave, with no recourse even to the church, which in fact commands that you must obey your massa. The Bible did not only accept slavery; it promoted it. One part of the Bible says, "Your male and female slaves are to come from the nations around you; from them you may buy slaves. You may also buy some of the temporary residents living among you and members of their clans born in your country, and they will be your property. You can bequeath them to your children as inherited property and can make them slaves for life" (Leviticus 25:44–46). And in Exodus 21:20–21, the Bible says, "Anyone who beats their male or female slave with a rod must be punished if the slave dies as a direct result, but they are not to be punished if the slave recovers after a day or two, since the slave is their property." The priest then comes to you and, in his usual sanctimonious voice, expresses his sympathy for you. He tries to comfort you by saying that while you must obey your white massa on earth, there has been another white man somewhere who died for you so that when you die and go to heaven, you and massa will live alongside each other and eat at the same table. As a slave, all you can do is look at the priest and wonder at the convoluted nature of his gospel.

Even after emancipation, the African is pursued and haunted out of every opportunity to make a living for himself and family. The token forty acres and a mule that was given to thousands of former slaves is later snatched away and the recipients thrown into destitution. Slaves that acquired certain trade skills during slavery are blocked from opportunities to use them.

Slavery, the subjection of the people of African origin for the benefit of the white people has never ceased to exist but has, over time, evolved into less obvious and more subtle forms that still linger in the form of systematic or institutional racism. Systematic racism explains the disparities and inequities in America in the areas of education, housing, employment, and health care, among many others. Systematic racism provides some explanation to the ongoing problems in the criminal justice system and the racial disparities in the impact of the coronavirus pandemic. It is a very sad indictment on America that the country still has a president in the twenty-first century who, instead of being at the forefront of seeking to heal the country, cancels federal racial sensitivity training and threatens to defund schools for wanting to teach children about slavery, saying that such activities are un-American propaganda.

The African slavery, which some have referred to as the African holocaust, is probably the most egregious of all acts against humanity in the history of mankind. According to Marley K (August 10, 2019) estimates of the number of Africans who died during the transatlantic slave trade range from six to one hundred fifty million, and the official United Nations estimate is seventeen million. With some African Americans only a few generations removed from slavery, the impact of slavery is far from being just history. The deep structural racial inequalities and the traumas of displacement and disenfranchisement are real and reverberate throughout the years to this day in America. And yet the African Americans are the only group that has not received reparations for the state-sanctioned injustices against them, not even an apology from the American congress or federal government. Even the debate about reparations, which has been half-hearted and sporadic, is still at the very basic level. It is not yet about how much, when, where, or how but about if there should be any reparations at all!

There is a long history of formal apologies and compensation for state-sanctioned injustices against humanity. A well-known case of reparations is that of the Jewish holocaust, for which millions of dollars were paid and are still being paid to date. In the recent past, America has also issued reparations to various groups for injustices committed against them, including the Japanese American internment, the native land seizures, and the overthrow of the Kingdom of Hawaii. But there has been no political will to acknowledge, apologize, and to compensate the African Americans for the clearly obvious and most heinous of injustices to mankind, even as some of the slaveholders were compensated for loss of property at the time slavery was abolished! There have been all kinds of excuses for not considering the reparations for the African Americans. The excuses range from Mitch McConnell's "None of currently living" is responsible for slavery to the twisted logic that equates reparations with victimhood. Also, some people have the mistaken view of reparations as a black versus white issue. The irony of it all is that while it is every white person since slavery to now and beyond who benefits from slavery, the question of reparations becomes a national issue that requires everyone to participate in its resolution. Reparations are issued from the national purse to which everyone, including the victims of slavery, contribute. Kanda views reparations in a representation of two communities, one a slave community and the other a white community. For four hundred years, the slave community generates wealth not for itself but for the other, leaving the slave community and its descendants impoverished. On the other hand, for the same period of four hundred years, the white community consumes the slave-generated wealth by investing it in education, health care, housing, infrastructure, and into many other subsidies and services that benefit the whole white community and its future descendants, including Mitch Mcconnell. A slave child in the slave community is born in a slave cabin, attended to by an untrained midwife, if any at all. The white child in the white community, whatever his future views on slavery and race will be, is born surrounded by doctors and nurses under conditions made possible by the slave-generated wealth, and he and his descendants will continue to enjoy the benefits of this wealth and the white privilege that derives from it. Jon Greenberg (July 24, 2017) defines white privilege as "the reality that a white person's whiteness has come—and continues to come—with an array of benefits and advantages not shared by many people of color." What this means is that even the white people who fought against slavery, the abolitionists, were, not by their own choice nonetheless, beneficiaries of white privilege. The story of the slave community and white community offers some explanation to some estimates that today, according to Rashawn Ray and Andre M. Perry (April 15, 2020), a white family has roughly ten times the amount of wealth compared to an average black family. And it is that racial wealth gap that reparations are all about as an attempt to reduce the gap. If the Mcconnells of this world continue to keep their proverbial head in the sand, slavery will remain a festering wound and a sticky stain on the greatness and goodness of America.

REFLECTIONS

The opportunity to reflect back
From the sunset of one's life
Not given to many
Some, even more deserving
To Kanda, a life's blessing

There are people that loom large in Kanda's life. There is Tobias, Kanda's cousin and best childhood friend that he still misses even after so many years; *Mbuyanhini*, the grandmother every child loved at the village and one with a big heart to accommodate them all; Auntie D, a definition of love who treated Kanda as the son she never had; and Uncle James, who sent for Kanda at the village in order to give him a better life. It was Uncle James who gave Kanda his African nickname Kandashu, which for many years as he grew up, he did not like but has since become a proud part of his African identity. Another person that stands big in Kanda's life is his friend Robert. Without Robert and the help that his family extended to him, Kanda's life could have turned out very different without the opportunity to go to college. Kanda has maintained close contact with his friend and his sister Margaret.

There have also been several chance encounters that have had a significant impact on Kanda's life. Among these was the connection Kanda had with Charles through a mutual friend. It was through him that Kanda met his wife, and he has since become a valuable friend of the family who has always been there for Kanda and his family in times of happiness and periods of challenges. Kanda's chance encounter with Angela, who persuaded him to consider the job that her company was recruiting for, landed Kanda in the Reserve Bank of Zimbabwe, which became his best employer for the greater part of his working life. The sharing of a desk on his first day of high school ended with a friendship that provided Kanda with a bridge to cross to a life that would have been different without college education. Kanda's casual encounter with the young man from the President's Office led Kanda to flee his home in Zimbabwe to become a citizen of the greatest country in the world.

Kanda is a product of many sacrifices. He can still remember seeing his parents toiling in the vegetable garden that he also worked in. His mother used to be laughed at by some of the villagers for wearing old clothes with holes and patches all over as she saved every penny for Kanda and his siblings. Kanda's father traveled more than six hundred kilometers to seek admission for his son at Tegwani Institute in Plumtree. He walked the distance from Plumtree town to the Tegwani Mission and back, even as he was limping from a chronic leg problem. Kanda's sister Getrude never worked much for herself as she had to help the parents to provide for Kanda and the other siblings. During Kanda's final year at Tegwani in 1966, when Getrude got married and was pregnant, she delayed taking time off from her job and continued to work when she was heavy with child in order to see Kanda through high school. The greatest sacrifice for Kanda and the rest of the family was, however, born by Kanda's younger sisters, Mavis and Florence who had to forfeit school at a young age in order to take care of siblings when the parents fled home due to politics. That sacrifice is unmeasurable in terms of its long-term impact on their lives.

Kanda is very happy with his life this far. He is happy that he has been able to fulfil his parents' expectations that he grows up a God-fearing person and that he gets some education that would provide him with the tools to deal with many of life's challenges. He is proud that he has been able to be of help to his family from the time when he was still a student and continued to do so for his mother, who passed on at the age of ninety-eight. Kanda has given his wife and children a decent life, living in safe neighborhoods and sending his children to the best schools in Zimbabwe. He has provided his children with the opportunities to live their dreams. Kanda has also been able to give back to the village that helped in his upbringing. He has been very satisfied with his career in working and helping people. Kanda and his family are proud of the scholarship fund that they set up in honor of Kanda's father, which pays the school fees for four students at Rutope Secondary School each year. The family plans to increase the fund to cater for six students at the school per year. The Rutope Secondary School is the senior school to Chindotwe Primary School, which was founded by Kanda's father. Kanda is also now very proud that he has been able to write his own story in his own way rather than leave it to be told by others in their own peculiar ways.

It is human nature to always want more in life. Kanda had some dreams that he was unable to fulfil but is now enjoying through his children. He had dreamed so much about becoming a medical doctor and had secured a provisional university admission for it, which he failed to qualify for. He now lives that dream through his daughter Kuda, who is now a medical doctor. Kanda had attempted many business ventures, which never came to much. His son Tatenda studied for a business degree, and his long-term goal is to establish his own business, and Kanda believes that where he failed to succeed, his son will. Kanda grew up valuing education so much that had he had the opportunity, he would have wanted to pursue it to its highest level, with his eye on that coveted PhD beret. He now puts on the beret through his daughter Mutsa, Doctor of International Psychology.

Kanda's world view has expanded and changed with time. Among the outstanding items on his bucket list is a visit to Australia, the only one of the five continents of the world that he is still to visit. Kanda has observed that there are many similarities among people of different countries, races, and cultures. The differences only serve to add color and richness to the range of diversity. While there may be all these differences and conflicts among racial groups, Kanda sees an underlying trend whereby the divergent colors will gradually become blurred, leading to a more united and consolidated human race in harmony with itself.

Kanda has learned that, in Africa at least, political freedom can be a mirage, an illusion. In Zimbabwe, as elsewhere on the continent, people believed that by removing the oppressive white colonial government, they would live a better life. Many people suffered and sacrificed their lives for that cause, only to end up in a worse situation. The change from colonial white government to the black government was quite significant in that while the former oppressed one section of the community, the black for the benefit of the other, the white, the incoming black government oppressed both communities for the benefit of itself alone. The new governing elite expropriated the resources of the country for its own satisfaction at the expense of the rest of the nation. In the extreme case of dictatorship, everything is for the sole benefit of the dictator. That is the situation that Zimbabwe has been for many years now, first under Robert Mugabe and then under Emmerson Mnangagwa. Nearly a quarter of Zimbabwe's population has fled the country, with many families separated and scattered all over the world. The majority of all those that have remained in the country live under extreme poverty in addition to widespread physical and mental injustices as the dictatorship seeks to suppress dissent. Zimbabwe and Africa as a whole appear to be under some curse, which turns their liberators into monsters that feed on their own. Kanda's family suffered a great deal under the white colonial regime, with his parents forced to flee from their home and family, the family home and property destroyed, and some of Kanda's siblings having to drop out of school. Kanda and his family are going through similar and sometimes worse circumstances under a black government, forcing Kanda, his wife, and children to live in exile away from their beloved country. The tragedy of Zimbabwe is that Robert Mugabe, who first brought this suffering on Zimbabwe, died without facing justice for his atrocities. The people of Zimbabwe hope that Mugabe's successors, who are more evil than even him, will not be as lucky to escape justice.

The biggest change in Kanda's life over the years has been in an area that he finds difficult to explain clearly, his Christian faith. He is relieved that he did not become a priest because he would have had to quit the priesthood or continue his work in the church without the full conviction of faith because of growing doubts due to contradictions and distortions in the Christian teaching. Kanda has now come to value all attempts by man to reach and connect with their Creator in their own different ways. Thus, he now values all religions equally and does not believe that there is any one religion that is superior to all others or one that can be said to be the only way to God as claimed by Christianity and other religions. Kanda's conception of the all-embracing God is of a God that has provided every group of people in his creation with a way to reach and connect with him, with ways that may not necessarily be the same for all his people. No group of people has a monopoly of God, and any religion that claims that monopoly is guilty of blasphemy. At one time, Kanda and his wife were unfortunate to be the only black people in a white church congregation when their pastor, a very well-respected priest who must have temporarily forgotten about their presence, made a remark to the congregation to the effect of "how blessed we are, we the blond and blue-eyed like the son of God himself!" No one group of people can expropriate God from all his other people. This appears to be the problem with most religions and more so with the Christian church, in which among many of its many denominations and numerous sects, each claims to be the only true church of God, and many believe white people are the only true children of God.

The way the Bible was written and Christianity do not reflect a universal perspective. There is clearly a cultural and time-bound context in which the Bible was written. There are instances too where you can see the hand of man, as opposed to the spiritual, in the portrayal of God, which resulted in one theologian named Reverend Canaan Banana in a Zimbabwean newspaper in May 1991, challenging Christian scholars "to seriously consider rewriting the Bible so that God can be liberated from dogmas of ethnic syndicates." To accept that Jews are a chosen people, God's preferred group of people among all nations, defeats the core teaching of Christianity and of the whole Bible. And there are Christians today who, through songs, express a yearning to go to Jerusalem when they die when all they really need is a visa and airfares to get to Jerusalem in the Middle East! The unanswered question is shouldn't all religions seek to establish a more universal perspective rather than each insisting on its narrow view? Shouldn't they be more accommodative rather than exclusive?

For Kanda, this has been one of the major failures of Christianity. During colonization, Christianity was used as a civilizing tool that sought to separate the native peoples from their cultures and religion without any attempt to accommodate, corroborate, and build on those cultures and religions. Kanda grew up under Christianity in his own native country without any benefit of choice for his own people's religion, which was destroyed during the civilizing crusade. Why should we be talking all the time about the important religious people among the Jews with no mention anywhere at all about, say, Zimbabwe's own great spirit medium, Mbuya Nehanda?

The Bible as the Word of God should be eternal and not be subject to tinkering at the whim of man. The fact that the Bible was compiled by a group of men, some of whom not necessarily religious people, from a small selection among many writings raises questions about the final product being a true representation of the Word of God. The recent calls to rewrite the Bible in order to include other cultural and ethnic perspectives speaks to the parochial nature of the Bible as written. The tinkering of the Bible, approved by Pope Francis to change the Lord's Prayer, which is attributed to Jesus Christ himself from saying "lead us not into temptation" to "do not let us fall into temptation," puts to question the infallibility of the Bible as the true Word of God. This distortion is compounded by recent calls by progressive theologians and Christian scholars to revise parts of the Bible that no longer conform to today's view of political correctness or are now out of context of current worldview. In all this, you begin to see the hand of man over the supposedly Word of God. And when you hear those that lead the church start calling themselves holy and assigning themselves titles like "Your Holiness," everyone's antenna needs to shoot up because no man of the flesh is ever completely free of human transgressions that require redemption. The scandalous child sexual abuse, which has been widespread in the Roman Catholic church, belies the holiness being claimed.

Kanda also finds the story of Jesus confusing. He wonders how God could send his Son to one tiny geographic spot in his vast creation when, with all his powers, he could have easily made it possible for Jesus to show himself and interact with all of God's people wherever they were on earth. To add to this, the people among whom Jesus was born and lived, people who should know him or about him the best and who should be witness to the rest of the world, do not recognize and acknowledge him as the Son of God. The coming of the Son of God, Jesus the Messiah, was heralded by Jewish prophets. According to Jewish theology, the coming of the Messiah was to be accompanied by a specific series of events, none of which occurred during the lifetime of Jesus nor afterward. The Jews believe that the Messiah is still to come and that the worship of Jesus is a form of idolatry, which should be forbidden. They view Jesus as having been the most influential and, consequently, the most damaging of all false prophets. This is the view of the people that the Bible says are the chosen ones of God.

Kanda was born and brought up as a Christian, the only religion that was available to him after the indigenous people's way of worship was destroyed by the colonizers and their missionaries. Kanda would probably have been a Muslim had he been born in a Muslim country or a follower of Buddha if he had been born in India. He is, however, grateful to the Christian teaching, which molded his character and values, and for the many social and materials benefits he has received over the course of his life. He will continue to go to church whenever he can and will continue to pray the only way he knows how. He regards the Lord's Prayer, which is attributed to Jesus, to be universal in content. He wishes he had had the opportunity to be exposed to the many other religions. What has, however, changed fundamentally in Kanda in recent years is an awakening, a realization of something that had been lodged deep inside him without him being aware of it—the sense of loss from being forcibly disengaged from his people's spiritual being and their way to Mwari. It is a feeling that is difficult to describe. To put it simply, it is like the case of a goat that is brought up as a pig and is happy in that life, only to realize one day that he is not in fact a pig but a goat. The goat must feel like it has been cheated out of his real identity all those years. It is a very unsettling state of being, and that is where Kanda is in his search for his true identity. At the very deep level of his being, as he contemplates his approaching departure from this earth, he now feels more and more connected with his Grandpa Chitate and all those gone before him, the ancestors who will receive him, intercede for his failings on earth, and lead him to his Mwari. Kanda has a Sahwira, Muturikwa, at the village. Sahwira is a special kind of friendship in Kanda's tradition. Kanda has arranged with the Sahwira that upon his death, wherever that would be and aside from the burial ceremony that Kanda's family would conduct in accordance with Kanda's life as a Christian, the Sahwira will perform a special rite for him. The Sahwira will, in the privacy of his home, play a few strands on his African mbira musical instrument accompanied by a word or two of *detembo* (supplication), entreating Kanda's ancestors to receive their son. Kanda is finally free of the Christianity's conundrum about whether the slave and massa will indeed one day live alongside each other and eat on the same table!

EPILOGUE

You cannot introduce yourself to others unless you know your name.

In a saying attributed to Jose Marti, a Cuban revolutionary and poet, every man should plant a tree, have a child, and write a book. The rationale behind it is that these all live on after us, thus ensuring a measure of immortality. I have planted many trees in my life and continue to do so. I have had children who now have their own children. And I have finally written a book. I have wanted, for a long time, to write a book. Over the years, I have considered all kinds of titles, such as *Every Life Has a Story, The Son of the Soil, The Motherland, Affinity with Nature,* and many others. At the end of the day, however, I came back to the subject closest to me—ME. Once I was decided on that subject, I was faced with the question "What then about me?" leading to "Who is me? Who am I?" It is this question that has led me on this long journey in search of myself, a lonely and intricate venture with no guide. I have learned that to search for one's self is not to separate from others, to exclude the other people. Rather, it is to seek to know oneself first in the diversity of many others. You cannot introduce yourself to other people and interact meaningfully with them unless you know who you are.

The theme of my story, the search for myself, was born of my birth between two divergent religions, two competing cultural narratives with my father on one side and my grandpa, the family patriarch, on the other. Those present wondered whether or not that circumstance of my birth was a curse or a double blessing, a question that has followed and nagged me on my journey: am I my father's representation or my grandpa's? As I proceeded on my journey, with some pieces of the puzzle beginning to fall into place, my questioning started to shift. I started to ask myself whether it had to be one or the other, and that is what finally led me to the discovery that at the end of the day, I was in fact the protégé of both my father and my grandpa. My grandpa's approach was direct, while that of my father was more circuitous, realizing the complexities of modern life and equipping me with the tools to navigate through and back to where I should be—the place where my grandpa wanted me to be from the very beginning. I am at peace now and for all the remaining days of my life on this earth.

ABOUT THE AUTHOR

The author is the first son in a family of eight children. He was born and grew up in colonial Rhodesia, now Zimbabwe. He learned early in life to take care of himself and his younger siblings when his parents fled their home at the village due to nationalist politics. The author attended Methodist mission schools up to high school and studied social work at the University of Zimbabwe's School of Social Work. He also obtained master's degrees in manpower studies and in business administration (MBA) much later in life. His early working life was characterized by a number of challenging jobs in which he was either the youngest or the first black person in the job. He retired from his last job in Zimbabwe as advisor to the governor of the Reserve Bank of Zimbabwe in 2002. In 2003, he and his family had to leave Zimbabwe for political reasons. The family settled in the United States of America, where they currently reside in Dallas, Texas.

CPSIA information can be obtained
at www.ICGtesting.com
Printed in the USA
LVHW011146211121
703954LV00005B/72